(DON'T) CALL ME CRAZY

ALSO EDITED BY KELLY JENSEN

HERE WE ARE: FEMINISM FOR THE REAL WORLD

(DON'T) CALL ME CRAZY

33 Voices
START THE
CONVERSATION ABOUT
MENTAL HEALTH

EDITED BY
KELLY JENSEN

ALGONQUIN 2018

Published by Algonquin Young Readers
an imprint of Algonquin Books of Chapel Hill
Post Office Box 2225
Chapel Hill, North Carolina 27515-2225

a division of Workman Publishing
225 Varick Street
New York, New York 10014

Book design by Laura Palese.

Grateful acknowledgment is made to the holders of
copyright, publishers, or representatives on pages 224–225, which constitute
an extension of the copyright page.

Library of Congress Cataloging-in-Publication Data
Names: Jensen, Kelly, editor.
Title: (Don't) call me crazy : 33 voices start the conversation about mental health /
edited by Kelly Jensen.
Description: First edition. | Chapel Hill, North Carolina :
Algonquin Young Readers, 2018. | Audience: Age 14–18. |
Audience: Grade 9 to 12. | Includes bibliographical references.
Identifiers: LCCN 2018010861 | ISBN 9781616207816
(trade pbk. original : alk. paper)
Subjects: LCSH: Mental illness—Case studies. | Mental health—Case studies. |
CYAC: Mental health—Case studies. | Young adults—Mental health—Case studies.
Classification: LCC RC509.8.D66 2018 | DDC 616.89/0092l—dcsh
LC record available at https://lccn.loc.gov/2018010861

10 9 8 7 6 5 4 3 2 1
First Edition

FOR THOSE WHO
HAVE FOUND THEIR
BRAVE AND FOR
THOSE WHO ARE
STILL **LOOKING**

TABLE OF

CONTENTS

CHAPTER 2

WHERE "CRAZY" MEETS CULTURE

CHAPTER 3
THE MIND-BODY CONNECTION

CHAPTER 4
BEYOND STRESS AND SADNESS

CHAPTER 5
TO BE OKAY

INTRODUCTION

WE ALL HAVE THOUGHTS, FEELINGS, and internal struggles. They're all part of what makes us human. Our brains are complex, intricate, and unbelievably fascinating machines that serve as central command for our bodies and our lives day in and day out.

And yet, we don't talk about our brains as much as we should. Mental health is a core component of our overall health, but finding ways to talk about it comes far less naturally—and can be far less accepted—than talking about our physical health.

(Don't) Call Me Crazy is a conversation starter and guide to better understanding how and where mental health impacts us each and every day. This is neither a tool for diagnosis nor a medical guide. It's a pulling back of the curtain and an opportunity to get up close and personal with mental health. It is by turns intense and raw, as well as humorous and lighthearted. It showcases a wide range of experiences, as well as the power and eccentricities of each person's unique brain.

CHAPTER ONE

WHAT'S "CRAZY"?

IS THERE A SINGLE DEFINITION of what it means to be "crazy"? Is using the word "crazy" offensive to those struggling with mental illness and something to be avoided? What does it mean for people when labels like "crazy" are attached to their everyday experiences?

One of the best ways to understand mental health is, of course, to start talking about it. The more we talk, the more it becomes clear that there's no single definition of "crazy," that there's no single experience of "crazy," and that the word "crazy" itself means different things to different people. Some avoid labels, while others embrace them. There is power in language, and there's power in what a word or a label can mean to each person.

"Crazy" is not a singular—or definitive—experience.

DEFYING DEFINITION

by Shaun David Hutchinson

I have Doctor Who shoes. They're custom-made Converse high-tops that I created online. They're TARDIS blue with white detailing and a black strip down the back that says Police Box. I love those shoes and I wear them everywhere.

I am not, however, the Doctor.

My profession is that of author. I spend most days clacking away on a keyboard (another custom-made job, but one I built myself, with old-timey typewriter keys and a hardwood case), drinking coffee, and talking to my dog. Over the past six years, I have produced an average of two books per year, and all the subject matter I write about is very personal to me.

I am not, however, my books.

Many of my off-hours (and often when I have a day job) are spent working with computers. Programming, building hardware, tinkering. I learned to build computers when I was sixteen. I wrote my first bit of code when I was twenty. I have supported myself throughout the years working with computers, and I've enjoyed being able to make money doing something I love.

I am not, however, a computer.

When I was nineteen, I attempted suicide. I was diagnosed with a major depressive episode. I have since been diagnosed as having persistent depressive disorder. I just call it depression. Some days are better than others. Some *years* are better than others. When everything else in my life is going well, I know I'm about to go through an episode because I'll begin to feel like I'm getting the flu. I become achy, exhausted, irritable. I have tried many different medications over the years but haven't found one that works for me. I have come to accept that I will deal with depression for the rest of my life.

I am not, however, depression.

Depression does not define me. If I were to make a list of all the words I, or others, might use to describe me, it might include: "weird," "inconsiderate," "quiet," "lonely," "goofy," "kind," "awkward," "focused," and "depressed." But those are simply different facets of the person people see when they see me. Depending on the time of day or whether I've had enough coffee or am on a deadline, a hundred people might walk away with an entirely different set of words they'd use to describe me. And while all those words might be useful for cataloging my behavior in one given circumstance, they would not and could not define me completely. Because we define words, not people.

We define words. We use words to define *other* words. A single word can have multiple meanings depending upon context, but it remains a thing that can be defined. "Depression," for example, is a word with a definition. If you look up "depression" in the *Diagnostic and Statistical Manual of Mental Disorders (DSM-5)*, you'll find a list of valuable criteria necessary for diagnosing depression. Look the word up in the dictionary, and you'll find it defined in simpler terms. I have my own definition of "depression" based on my personal experiences with it, because "depression" is a word, and we define words, not the other way around.

Depression is a thing I carry with me. It is a shadow that lurks inside me. Depression is the smoke that ebbs and flows within my body. Depression is the result of chemical changes within my brain. Depression is the parasite. It is the foreign invader. An unwelcome guest. Depression is the voice that whispers in the back of my head. It is the rain that falls and the thunder that shakes the windows and the lightning that strikes the earth.

It is the ghost that haunts me.

I define "depression," but depression does not define me because you cannot define a person. Not with a single word, not with an entire book. Human beings defy definition. Yet the stigma surrounding mental illness makes some believe we *can* use it to define others, and it often deceives us into believing we must use it to define ourselves.

I dislike the word "hysterical." It is derived from the Latin word *hystericus* (of the womb) and is often used as a means to undermine women. Men wield the word like a cudgel to undercut women and diminish the legitimacy of any argument they might make. And the tactic frequently works because even those who might not be aware of the word's etymology at least subconsciously know that it (falsely) implies weakness they believe to be applicable only to women. Calling a woman hysterical is a despicable attempt to devalue her and any argument she might be making by defining her by a single characteristic.

People use "depression" in a similar manner.

I wear glasses, I have attention deficit hyperactivity disorder (ADHD), I battle persistent headaches, I am allergic to dust, I have depression. I am no more shy about discussing my depression than I am about discussing my glasses or my headaches. I talk more openly about depression because I hope to show others, especially teens, that depression is not a terminal disease. As a result, most of the people who regularly interact with me know I have depression. Most understand that it is simply a fact of my life. A thing I deal with. Some, however, attempt to use it as a weapon to define—and sometimes undermine—me.

To say my twenties were a tumultuous time is something of an understatement. I moved around frequently, desperate to find my place in the world. I dated a guy during that time, and our relationship was combative from the start. He could be kind and funny. We would often drive along the beach road on Palm Beach island and tell each other increasingly horrifying stories about the people who lived in the gaudy mansions we passed. I was madly in love with him, and I do believe he loved me in his own weird way. But we fought frequently. I was insecure and clingy; he was unsure where I fit into his life.

It was during that time that I was also seeing a psychiatrist in one of my many attempts to find a medication to help me control the symptoms of my depression. Some of those medications made me sleep for twenty hours a day, while others seemed to have no effect at all. During one of our arguments, over what I can no longer recall, my boyfriend-at-the-time said, "You need to go get your medication adjusted."

Just like that, he'd delegitimized my argument and defined me by my depression. It wasn't me speaking—it was my depression. It wasn't me packing my bags—it was my depression. I wasn't me. I was my depression.

In 2016, I gave a speech at *School Library Journal*'s Leadership Summit about the ways in which books can be bridges, and how they can help us empathize and understand people whose experiences are different from our own. During the speech, I spoke openly and frankly about my struggles with depression and how I use them to shape the books I write. I was and still am pretty proud of that speech, and when *School Library Journal* posted the video of it online, I shared it across social media. I was working at the time for a company where I was involved in computer programming. My boss was an interesting guy that I'd become friends with. He stumbled upon the video of my speech, which he complimented me on. And that, I assumed, was that.

A few weeks later, I was venting to him about an issue I was having with a member of our team—typical office politics that had gotten on my nerves. And while I'm not shy about expressing my opinions, I also dislike pointing out problems unless I am also going to offer a solution. So I did that. I vented. I proposed a fix. And I thought I'd made my point. Then, as I was leaving, he said, "You going to be all right? You're not going to kill yourself over this, are you?"

I didn't know what to say. He couldn't have stolen my voice any more effectively if he'd yanked out my tongue with a pair of pliers and cut it off with gardening shears. With that one question, he had reduced me and my argument to nothing more than my mental illness. He had defined me by my depression. I spent the rest of my time working there knowing that any time I offered my opinion or brought up a complaint, he would attribute my words not to me but to my mental illness.

Society continues to see mental illness as a person-defining trait. When some people find out you have depression, suddenly every action—past, present, and future—becomes attributable to the disease and not to you as a person. Your actions are no longer your own. Your words are no longer your own. They become the actions and words of depression, and you become something less than human. Which is

YOU MAY KNOW SOMEONE WITH A MENTAL ILLNESS BUT THEY ARE **NOT** THAT MENTAL ILLNESS.

ludicrous. When I had my gallbladder removed in 2010, no one dismissed me because a part of my digestive system was faulty. No one listened to something I had to say and responded, "He can't be trusted—he doesn't have a gallbladder." Yet this happens all too frequently with those who live with mental illness. We are dismissed, distrusted, told our thoughts are not our own.

And the most fucked-up part is that once someone has defined you by your mental illness enough times, you begin to define yourself by it. Depression is a pathological liar. I've published six books and have many more scheduled to come out. Yet my brain will spend hours telling me that I'm a shitty writer. That every sale, every good review is a fluke. That I should give up and spend the rest of my life working with computers in a cubicle. I spent a large chunk of my twenties and thirties doubting myself. I questioned whether the strangers and friends and family members who had ascribed my words and actions to my depression were right. I spent hours awake at night replaying every facet of my day and wondering if I'd only done or said certain things because of my mental illness—and in doing so, I undermined my own sense of self. And when others so readily blamed my actions and words on depression, it made it more difficult for me to separate the truth from the lies within my own brain. If all those people were right, then maybe the things my brain was saying were right, too.

It's only been in the past few years that I've regained the ability to definitively say that my actions are my own. That my words belong to me. That I am not depression. Reaching this point has not been easy, and it's a process that never ends. There was no huge defining moment for me when I recognized how to change. It was a slow realization over many years. But the most important step for me was learning how to filter out the voices that didn't matter from the ones that did. Because the insidious trap of depression is that it tells you that either everything everyone says is right or everything everyone says is wrong. If a friend says I'm a good writer, and I believe them, then when a coworker says I'm overreacting because of my depression, I must believe them, too. Only that's not true. People lie, just like my own brain does. Learning who is trying to help me and who is simply trying to define me has allowed me to better see when my brain is lying to me and when it is telling the truth.

Taking back my life has happened in many other smaller ways, as well. It has required finding confidence in myself. And, honestly, I had to fake that *a lot* in the beginning. Sometimes I still have to fake it now. I've heard that liars often tell a lie so frequently that they begin to believe it. I've learned that combating a lie with the truth works in the same way. I keep repeating that my actions are my own, that I am worthwhile, that I am not the result of my depression, that I deserve to live. I tell myself those things daily to counteract the lies depression tells. Each time someone attempts to attribute my actions or words to my mental illness, I stop and tell myself that they are wrong.

A support system is crucial to the process. Friends, family members, anyone who cares about you. It might sound cliché, but my mother is a touchstone for me. When I'm not sure I can trust myself, I'll call her to talk things over because I know that I *can* trust what she says. To my mother, I am not the Doctor or a computer or my books or depression or even simply her son. I am a whole person: complex and unique and loved. She doesn't define me; she accepts me.

You may know someone who has a mental illness, but that person is *not* that mental illness. Don't try to tell them they are. You may have depression, but you are *not* depression. Stop telling yourself you are. Wake up every day and tell yourself that your thoughts and your words belong to you. No one is allowed to undermine who you are by defining you on their terms. Depression is a disease, a collection of symptoms. It is not a human being. It is not a person. It may live in your skin, but it does not control you. It may whisper in your ear, but it doesn't speak for you. It may be the smoke in your body, but it cannot suffocate you. It may be the result of chemical changes in your brain, but so is hunger. It may haunt you, but it will never drive you away.

Define words, not people. Define "depression," but don't define others by it. Because we are people and we defy definition.

DEFINING THE THING IS THE TRICK

by Ashley Holstrom

TRICHOTILLOMANIA

[trik-uh-til-uh-MEY-nee-uh]

(NOUN) a compulsion to pull out one's hair

I don't remember the first time my hand reached to my eyebrow and pulled. I don't know how much I'd ripped out before I looked down at my book and saw the pages speckled with eyebrow confetti. I don't know how long I'd been doing it when my mom walked in, squinted at me, and asked where my eyebrows went.

What I do remember is that jock asking when a clown with too much makeup joined the seventh grade. Those girls in health class asking what the hell was up with my face. Kids always, always asking if I had cancer.

I remember struggling to color on eyebrows, using pencils that turned orange on my pale skin. I remember feeling like I was the only person who did this thing and couldn't stop. I remember a therapist telling me her favorite mental illness is "trichotillomania" because the word is fun to say.

I remember Jeff, in trigonometry, who said he didn't know what was wrong with him, but every day in class, his eyelashes would disappear. We sat in the dreaded front row, our heads down until the bell rang. As I packed my bag, he'd brush eyelashes off his notebook. I told him the name of what he was doing and that I did it, too. He was the first person I met who faced "trich" with me. He signed my yearbook with: *Thanks for helping me with my eyelash problem. I'm going to really try and not pull them out. Really.*

Trichotillomania. Compulsive hair pulling. Its sister, dermatillomania, is compulsive skin picking. They fall under the umbrella of body-focused repetitive behaviors, a group of disorders that causes people to touch their hair, skin, and nails in ways that (usually) cause physical damage.

Some people go for the hair on their head; others go for eyebrows, eyelashes, pubic hair, arm hair, leg hair, nose hair, facial hair, any hair. Sometimes the urge is brought on by stress; other times, it's simply a relaxation method that's used while doing something mindless: reading, driving, watching TV, doing homework, scrolling through the internet for hours on end.

For me, the more I read, the fewer eyebrows and eyelashes I have. When I run out of hair in those places and/or get calluses on my fingertips from my nails digging in with each pull, I go for the hair on my head. Other times I pick at my scalp or find little scabs on my legs. As I drive home from work at midnight, in the comfort of the dark—and of being the only car on the highway—I run my hands over my face to find any imperfections that appeared during the day.

In my head, I'm cleansing my body. Never mind that my hands are gross and I'm spreading bacteria. That's not the point. The satisfaction of ridding my body of a flake of skin, a particularly clumpy bunch of mascaraed eyelashes, or an unruly eyebrow is all I'm after. A high, sort of. A comfort. Bonus: When I pull out my hair, sometimes I create a little sore that will soon scab over, and now there's more to pick. The cycle never ends.

My life has always been full of these compulsions. I sucked my thumb until I was eight. I had a baby blanket that I sniffed, rubbed, and carried with me at all times. I painted my nails religiously, then picked off the polish within a day. Those habits were "normal." This hair-pulling thing, not so much.

After puberty hit, I only did these things in private. Big kids don't suck their thumbs. Big kids don't pick their noses. Big kids don't carry their blankies with them everywhere. Big kids don't pull out their hair strand by strand.

. . .

TRICHSTER

[TRIK-ster]

(NOUN) a person who suffers from trichotillomania

When a trichster tells someone about what they do, they're bombarded with the usual refrains: "Dude, why?" or "Well, just . . . Stop" or "Put hot sauce on your hands." There are endless options for distracting yourself or keeping your hands busy doing something else. Fidget toys, spinner rings, Silly Putty. Peeling oranges, knitting, popping Bubble Wrap. But these distractions are bandages. They're temporary. They cover up the problem. They help you heal, momentarily, but they don't cure you.

Most sources say there is no cure for trich. Sorry. Get yourself a disorder that's curable next time. But—haha!—don't pull out your hair over it.

"But, girl, doesn't it hurt? I can't even bear getting my brows waxed."

No. It's like scratching an itch. I'm sure the first few pulls hurt, but those days are long gone.

"Is it an anxiety thing?"

That's what people think, but it's not, really. It's a mindless compulsion.

"Isn't it a form of self-harm?"

I guess.

"Don't you hate it?"

Every. Single. Day.

I've tried to quit more times than I can count. At times, I've stopped without realizing it.

It started to snowball in junior high. I was an angsty kid, bullied for being quiet and preferring the comfort of books over humans. As I read the Harry Potter books, I lost more eyebrows. *Harry Potter and the Order of the Phoenix* came out after I'd acquired a nasty sunburn, and between peeling away the dead skin on my shoulders and pulling out my eyebrows, I was set. When I reread the book a few months later, I noticed just how many eyebrow hairs I'd pulled out, seeing them nestled in the binding of the hardcover. I brushed them out and let them float away.

When my mom started to notice my once-envious brows were deteriorating, she couldn't understand why. Where were they going? Why were they disappearing more and more every day? How come my eyebrows looked curly after I'd been reading for a while?

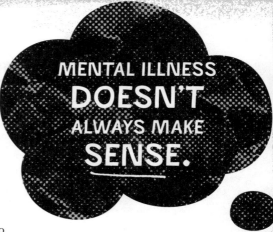

Her questions felt like an invasion. This was my thing I did in private, but I should have known that moms know everything. She scrutinized my face daily. When I gathered the courage to tell her I was pulling my eyebrows out with my fingers, but didn't know why, she asked what she could do to help. She would tell me to stop when she walked past my reading place. She would investigate when she sat next to me on the couch or gave me a hug when I left for school.

But she wanted to actively help, and decided to try a different route: makeup.

She helped me fill in the missing eyebrows. She had a stockpile of old eyebrow pencils she'd given up on after drawing on her brows for years—her once-fashionable pencil-thin brows stopped growing back, and she had just a few hairs above each eye. Those pencils became my battle armor, albeit with slightly mismatched colors.

But it was fine. I was merely filling in the missing hairs, not drawing on completely new eyebrows. Yet.

Things were calm for a while. My brows were mostly untouched for all four years of high school. I was reading more, which should have led to more pulling, but I guess the thrills and chills of those years distracted me.

For the first time in so long, I had full eyebrows—two whole eyebrows.

They stuck around for most of college, too. Another miracle.

In my final semester, though, life and schoolwork started to slow down. I had time to read for fun again. I went for some cute young adult romances to take my mind off having to enter the "real world" soon. And I started pulling again. By the time graduation rolled around, my eyebrows were gone, and I was too broke to buy an eyebrow pencil to cover up what I'd done. Oops.

Mental illness doesn't always make sense.

ENDURE

[en-DOOR]

(VERB) to bear with patience

What a way to start the first day of the rest of my life. I felt like a thirteen-year-old me again. And, fittingly, I moved back in with my parents, to the room where this whole thing began.

My pulling was the worst it had ever been. My regular reading spot was soon covered in hair. I sat on the disintegrating, Aztec-printed sofa by the front window, basking in the sun, reading every morning before heading to work. I'd run my fingers through my hair the whole time, catching knots and tangles, searching for wiry gray hairs, and letting the loose ones fall behind the dusty couch.

The vacuum may or may not have gotten clogged trying to clean up my hair. I tried to rationalize it: All this hair wasn't from one day. Hair is supposed to fall out. It's completely normal to lose up to a hundred hairs a day. Surely these are the hairs that would have come out on their own. Surely.

For the past few years, I've really focused on this thing I do. I want to *understand* it, not just hate myself for doing it. I've read every book on trichotillomania I can find—mostly books for psychiatrists with tips on helping patients with this disorder—but no matter how many times I read the tips and tricks, they don't sink in. An exercise might go something like this:

> *Count how many hairs you pull out. Keep track of that number and what you were doing, how you were feeling that day. Write down all the consequences of pulling out your hair—how much money does makeup or a wig cost to cover up what you've done? How does it make you feel? Disgusted? Ashamed? Focus on those feelings. Reverse them.*

I know exactly how much my makeup costs me. The good eyebrow pencils are eighteen dollars a pop, about once a month, which comes to $216 a year. Add in all the experiments with new pencils and tools that don't work, and over my lifetime, it's not a pretty sum to spend. (But at least my brows look good.)

I know exactly how I feel when I pull out an eyebrow hair and look at it and flick it away and say, "Okay, just one more," and then pull out another and say, "Just one more." I know I'm going to get up, look in the mirror, brush aside my bangs, and look at what I did to myself in an hour's time. I'll sigh, call myself a fucking idiot, run my fingers over my sparse brows, assess the damage. I'll use tweezers to pluck out any hairs that now don't fit the haphazard brow line my mindless hands created while I wasn't looking.

And counting the pulled hairs? That backfires. It turns into a game of trying to beat a high score.

I've tried making bets with myself: You can't get a new tattoo until you can go a month without pulling. You can't buy a new book until you can go a week without pulling. You can't splurge on a fancy coffee until you can go a morning without pulling. You can't, you can't, you can't.

When I told a therapist all this, she told me to stop beating myself up about it. "You don't seem like you want to quit," she said after I shook my head at her list of ways to control myself, "so stop trying." Reverse psychology? Maybe. It didn't work.

I didn't go back to therapy.

ON FLEEK

[on FLEEK]
(ADJECTIVE) on point, excellent, the bomb-diggity

God bless the trend to have wild eyebrows. Makeup artists post videos online showing off their extensive brow routines. Cosmetic stores sell packs of eyebrow stencils so that you can have different brows for every day of the week. Every makeup brand has a wide range of top-notch eyebrow tools. People notice eyebrows now, and compliments fly when they're "on fleek."

All the eyebrow love is bringing out the herds of trichsters. We go to the internet for companions, gathering on Tumblr, Twitter, and Instagram. We talk about our struggles and lift each other up. We are not alone. We are not disgusting.

I get to have fun with my eyebrows for the first time in my life. I get to have new eyebrows every day. Grumpy? Make them dark and bold. Sad? Make them blond and natural looking. Happy? Anything goes. I'm taking control of my mood by drawing whatever the heck I want above my eyes.

And I spend a lot of time on my drive to work wiggling my eyebrows at myself in the rear-view mirror. Deal with it.

ACCEPTANCE

[ak-SEP-tuhns]

(NOUN) the state of enduring without protest or reaction

Even though trichotillomania is a daily struggle, I find ways to laugh at it.

Hairstylists get a kick out of when I say, "Hey, whoa, hey, be careful with the shampoo—I don't have eyebrows. Please don't wipe them off." My guy rolls his eyes when he kisses my forehead and I say to be very, very careful with my eyebrows. Because I don't have any. In case he didn't know.

When a delivery person rings the buzzer and I only have one brow drawn on, I can't go down to get the package because I won't let my face with only one bangin' brow be seen by anyone.

I'm still pulling. If I'm not pulling, I'm twirling my hair. Or fidgeting with something. I probably will pull and fidget my whole life.

Trichotillomania used to control me, but now it's just a part of my existence. I can battle the effect, but the cause will always hang out in my brain somewhere. I'm still dealing with not being ashamed, but I'm getting there.

READING ABOUT
TRICH & MENTAL HEALTH

by Ashley Holstrom

FIVE BOOKS ABOUT TRICHOTILLOMANIA:

- *Marni: My True Story of Stress, Hair-Pulling, and Other Obsessions*
  by Marni Bates

- *Life Is Trichy: Memoir of a Mental Health Therapist with a Mental Health Disorder*
  by Lindsey M. Muller

- *Doesn't It Hurt?: Confessions of Compulsive Hair Pullers*
  by Sandy Rosenblatt (editor)

- *Help for Hair Pullers: Understanding and Coping with Trichotillomania*
  by Nancy J. Keuthen, Dan J. Stein, and Gary A. Christenson

- *Still Waiting: Hope for When God Doesn't Give You What You Want*
  by Ann Swindell

FIVE MENTAL HEALTH MEMOIRS:

- *Brain on Fire: My Month of Madness*
  by Susannah Cahalan

- *Willow Weep for Me: A Black Woman's Journey through Depression*
  by Meri Nana-Ama Danquah

- *Marbles: Mania, Depression, Michelangelo, and Me: A Graphic Memoir*
  by Ellen Forney

- *Haldol and Hyacinths: A Bipolar Life*
  by Melody Moezzi

- *Shadows in the Sun: Healing from Depression and Finding the Light Within*
  by Gayathri Ramprasad

WHAT I KNOW AND
WHAT I DON'T KNOW

by Dior Vargas

A few years ago, I gave myself the title: Latina Feminist Mental Health Activist.

Any time mental health is the subject of a film or movie, it mostly focuses on white people. The same thing happens when you google "mental illness" or "depression": the images that come up are of white people.

I live with mental illness and wanted to help others like me see themselves, so I started a photo project in 2014 that highlighted the lack of representation of people of color when it comes to the topic of mental illness. I asked people of color to send me images of themselves with a sign explaining what it means to them to live with a mental illness and how their illness is impacted by their different cultural experiences. The images came slowly at first, but as more people took part, the People of Color and Mental Illness Photo Project went viral, and it propelled me into the public spotlight. I was given opportunities that I never thought I would have. I went to the White House. I give speeches for organizations and at hospitals, colleges, and universities, and I've been interviewed for various news outlets. People come to me for advice, support, and guidance. The attention still feels surreal.

There were negative consequences to this, though. I experienced trolling and harassment from people who thought I was being racist and evil for excluding white people when all I wanted to do was highlight individuals with mental health issues who are rarely reflected in the media. It impacted my own mental health, as well.

I've always been insecure, and I struggle with impostor syndrome. To me, impostor syndrome is excelling at something or having good things happen in my career, paired with the sneaking suspicion that my good fortune will end because, ultimately, I don't deserve it. I can't revel in accolades or achievements because I feel I never truly deserve them. I don't know what the hell I'm doing, and sooner or later everyone will realize that. I can never enjoy the success of my work because I'm constantly worried that if I do enjoy it, I'll be put in my place and punished for thinking too highly of myself.

I often worry people will find out that I really don't know what I'm talking about. That I don't have it all figured out, either, and that I have many days where I can't bear to deal with what it means to live with mental illness. How can I be an advocate when I am still suffering? At times, I get tired of having mental health be such a big part of what I think about, what I talk about, and what I work on. It is what makes me different and what has caused me so much trauma put on center stage every single day.

Unfortunately, a few months after I started the photo project, I was laid off from

My name is Katharine & I am NOT defined by my mental illness, but I am grateful for what it has taught me.

my job. (It was actually the day after I posted a photo of myself.) I had been afraid for so much of my life, but this was a new kind of fear. How would I pay my bills? How could I go through a whole job search again?

What terrified me the most was not knowing what I would do about my health insurance. How would I pay for my mental health treatment? I felt screwed. I had to contend with the frustration of the Medicaid system. I quickly gave up and stopped treatment altogether.

While I searched for a new job, I made the decision to focus more on my project—I had this idea that if I found something that fulfilled me, like helping others through mental health advocacy, I would be all right—even if I wasn't able to help myself. The job hunt continued, but having something fulfilling to work on kept me active and engaged in my day-to-day life. Yet after a year of not undergoing any mental health treatment, I knew that I needed to take care of myself because my depression and anxiety weren't improving on their own. I eventually reconnected with a former therapist and started therapy again.

However, just when I thought that I had come to terms with my anxiety and depression and what they meant for me, I received a new diagnosis: borderline personality disorder (BPD). When I was initially diagnosed with depression years ago, I accepted it. Finally, there was a reason why I felt and acted in certain ways that others didn't. The diagnosis gave me an understanding of myself. However, with this additional diagnosis, despite how much work I'd done and the knowledge I had about mental illness, I fell apart. The sense of self that I had was taken away from me. I felt like I didn't know who I was anymore.

Not every diagnosis will elicit the same response. I had identified with my depression and anxiety so much and referenced it during so many talks, interviews, and conversations that it felt like my words were from a script. When I started my work as a mental health activist, I wanted to learn all that I could about mental health. Borderline personality disorder, though, was one illness that I never quite got to—one to which I didn't pay enough attention. Funny how that happens.

With the new diagnosis, I started researching everything I could about BPD. Most of what I found was extremely disparaging: I remember reading somewhere that people who have BPD fall between annoying and crazy and dangerous. I also read that those with BPD were broken down into types, and one group was witch/warlock. I found a Facebook post in which a woman said that she would rather work with ten people with schizophrenia than one person with BPD. I fell into a spiral of negativity. The information I found, compounded with the ever-present impostor syndrome, fed into what I've been good at doing for so long: treating myself like shit. My BPD diagnosis verified all my suspicions that I was a selfish, vile person. I began overanalyzing every single action I took and every single thought I had. This was my way of making sense of what I could. What hurt so much about BPD is that the diagnosis referred to my entire personality. I felt like it encompassed everything about me and should have been something I could control. When people who knew me told me they didn't believe I have BPD, the response made me feel a little better, but mostly it made me feel like I must have been good at hiding the truth. So this impostor syndrome felt all the more palpable and valid. I was so good at hiding my true, incompetent, flawed self. I fooled everyone.

Including myself.

Culturally, there are some mental illnesses we discuss more openly than others, like depression, anxiety, and bipolar disorder. They seem more digestible to the general public. This is not to say that they aren't debilitating or that there is a hierarchy to this pain, but these illnesses are usually the focus when we talk about mental health. Likewise, my community and background teaches that you are not supposed to talk about mental health issues and your personal struggles with them. They stay at home. The challenge of experiencing a new mental health diagnosis on top of what I was already comfortable with put me in a tough position in both my own head and my own community.

THIS IS ALL PART OF A **LEARNING** PROCESS.

The diagnosis was even harder for me because of my role as a mental health advocate.

People assume activists are doing well because of all they've accomplished. But this work can be draining, and when we don't take care of ourselves like we preach to others to do, we are no longer able to do what we are so passionate about. I have seen some of my fellow activists end their own lives. It is a daily fight for me to live another day and to fight for others who feel the same way.

I spent a year coming to terms with how I saw myself with my new diagnosis and what it meant for me and my activism—both personally and politically. I also wondered if I would ever talk publicly about my BPD. Then I learned from a different psychiatrist that I didn't have a full diagnosis of BPD. I just had aspects of it.

This news woke me up.

Mental illness is confusing, and it doesn't always make sense. Even though that year post-BPD diagnosis was torturous, it gave me the opportunity to learn more about myself and how labels influenced both the way I viewed myself and how I perceived what others thought of me. To me, that label of BPD meant that my feeling of being an impostor was true. That my paranoia about why things were going well for me was justified. I became focused on what the label BPD meant, but learning to rethink my beliefs about the complex experiences of mental illness and the labels attached to them made me realize something bigger about myself: While I allowed other people room to be who they were—messy, flawed, and complex—I didn't give myself that same leeway. Everything about me was in simple black and white.

Despite the characteristics detailed in the *Diagnostic and Statistical Manual of Mental Disorders* (*DSM-5*) for each mental illness, there is really nothing definite. People experience things differently. Everything is a shade of gray along a spectrum. But I struggle with applying this understanding to myself. My constant indecision and confusion coupled with my impostor syndrome made me yearn for black-and-white clarity, with less room for further, stressful interpretation about who I am and why I feel the way that I do.

Much of my work is to turn what can seem negative and draining into something positive and empowering. I needed to give myself the same compassion I try to help other people find for themselves, but I'm still learning and decolonizing my own mind. This is and will continue to be part of my life's work.

I'm choosing to set aside what the label of BPD may or may not mean. Being able to definitively say something, feel something, or do something without any hesitation or second guesses allows me a sense of control. That mode permits me to go against my consistent doubt. I've learned the hard way that labeling my BPD doesn't allow me to feel a sense of security, so I'd rather not think about it anymore. I'd rather keep getting up and getting to work.

While having a label for my experiences might strengthen the messages I deliver, if I don't know how to explain my illness to myself, I can't explain it to others. As a mental health advocate, trying to juggle those feelings only adds to my experience of impostor syndrome. I guess I'd rather live in ignorance than continue to stress about this label. Am I an impostor because I'm not willing to explore further who I truly am, or is it the self-care that I need in order to do the work that matters to me? Will I change my thinking about this in another year or two?

I don't know. This is all a part of the learning process.

What I do know is this: despite bouts with impostor syndrome, I'm a Latina Feminist Mental Health Activist. It's who I am now or, maybe, who I've always been. This is a label that I've chosen for myself. I'm not confused about what it means for me. It isn't a diagnosis, which doesn't always make perfect sense and may change over time or feel heavy on some days and nonexistent on others. I know what being a Latina Feminist Mental Health Activist is about and why I chose to be one. I'm happy with that choice.

WHAT'S, WELL, "CRAZY"?

by Sarah Hannah Gómez

Every year, on January 1, I would decide on a new style of handwriting for the coming year—maybe it was calligraphy-inspired or incorporated some cursive or involved a typewriter-like lowercase "a." I liked the idea of having something fresh for the new year.

I mentioned this personal tradition one year at camp and a girl said, offhand, "That's a mark of mental illness, you know. They can tell people have, like, schizophrenia or split personality disorder if their handwriting changes."

So I had, like, schizophrenia or something. Great.

We didn't really use "google" as a verb back then, even though the search engine was technically around by the time I was fourteen, but I googled the hell out of what it means to change your handwriting when I got home from camp. Schizophrenia came up a lot, which I was fairly certain I didn't have, yet the thought I might be crazy kept nagging me for years. But this research brought me to discover the "science" of graphology, which takes psychology and applies it to visual art interpretation. The way you dot your *i* or the size of the space between your letters might reveal something about you. Even if I didn't believe I had schizophrenia or everything I learned about graphology, I did come to understand handwriting could indicate certain neuromuscular disorders that affect the ability to steady your hand or send a signal from your brain to your pen.

But to me, that was beside the point. A girl at camp told me I was nuts because I liked restyling my handwriting, and I couldn't let that thought go. It was like being called crazy because you liked dyeing or cutting your hair into different styles, or because you liked wearing wild outfits. I wasn't just quirky. I was crazy.

The thing is, I did feel crazy. I felt crazy all the time. I was fourteen, and for at least four years, I had been angry about every little thing and nothing at all. I would get into screaming matches with my older sister and my parents. I was dramatic and had many feelings. I would rant in my online journal and spill my thoughts, naming every person I thought had wronged me, every person I had a crush on, every person I was jealous of. Any little thing could make me cry. My feelings of crazy weren't only emotional, though. They were physical, too. My stomach always hurt, and I caught every bug that went around. I could never breathe like a normal person. I learned later this was a combination of celiac disease, vocal cord dysfunction, and fibromyalgia; but at the time, experiencing these things without a name for them did not help my moods.

Online, I could be—and was—completely unrestrained in my emotions. Strangers who commented laughed about how melodramatic I was, while friends asked why I was so angry. I didn't think I was "angry," which to me meant wearing all black and listening to screamy music. I was just sharing my feelings, as fast and unfiltered as they came. I couldn't understand why people thought I was different, so *angry*, when I thought I was acting the same as everyone else my age did—writing confessionals on the internet.

At school, I was belligerent when I didn't like a subject or a teacher, and I spoke out of turn excitedly if there happened to be a topic I liked on any given day. I was a "good student" in the traditional sense of the term: I earned good grades and was accepted to every college I applied to. School wasn't a challenge to me, though, and it didn't take much hard work or engagement to do well. I wasn't invested in it.

In my free time, I gravitated toward movies and books about people doing drugs and people with mental illness, or, most often, media about people doing drugs to numb their mental illnesses. The foggy, blurred look of the cinematography and voice of the text went perfectly with the way I felt I was making my way through the world— sometimes moving through it like a blob and other times reexperiencing the same thing over and over and over, like déjà vu. Watching and reading those things made me feel edgy, too, and I was desperate to be cool and to have people notice me.

Around this time, I started to get the idea that I might have bipolar disorder, wondering if that might explain how I could have so much energy and enthusiasm, only to be dejected and try to hide away a few weeks later. I didn't know much about bipolar disorder, except that it was something I had learned about in movies and books, and that it had to do with feeling different from day to day. But as I began looking closer at what bipolar disorder was, the criteria did not fit me. I had to do something *really* wild, like run away or parachute out of a plane or get hooked on drugs to truly have the disease. Bipolar disorder was something other people had to notice, and nobody said I had anything other than anger issues. I was duly punished when I did something wrong and lost friends when I was cruel to them. That just made me a regular teenager. Nobody in my life told me I needed real help, only that I needed to shape up. Only that I had a persecution complex and needed to get over myself. Only that I should take a quaalude and calm down (said flippantly, the way many people reduce mental illness to nothing more than an annoying habit).

And yet I kept circling back to the thought that I must have something wrong with me because of *my handwriting*. Was I crazy? Was there something to that habit I couldn't see? Even later on in high school, when I dropped the tradition and just let my handwriting be what it wanted to be, I was hyperaware anytime a piece of my writing was more or less scribbly than usual, larger or smaller than usual, or otherwise *off*. What did it say about me? Would my teachers or family notice that the notes I left or the shopping lists I made looked different? Did they think I was crazy?

You know what that is? An obsessive behavior.

You know what mental illness I *do* have? Obsessive-compulsive disorder (OCD).

I was very resistant when a psychiatrist told me, almost as an afterthought, that I had OCD. That disorder was for people who counted ceiling tiles and kissed doorknobs twenty-two times every Tuesday; at least, that's how I'd always seen it (on TV, in books, in movies, in the media, etc.). I might double-check my alarm clock before bed, but that was it.

My mental illness wasn't OCD alone, though. Rather, OCD was the disorder that was "comorbid" with bipolar II disorder, the same illness that I suspected I'd had for years. It was confirmed my freshman year of college.

Bipolar II is the one that *doesn't* look like the movies. There is no skydiving or regular self-harm, but smaller, and often more frequent, shifts from mania (high energy) to depression and back again. Those periods when I didn't need to sleep very much, had frantic and chaotic thought and writing patterns, or would forget to eat

meals? Mania. Entering mid-February and feeling, without fail, like everything is hopeless
and exhausting and worthless for at least two
months? Depression. And that thing I did where
I would replay some embarrassing or enraging
thing that had happened previously over and
over for weeks? Sometimes still thinking about
it months later? Always worrying that I'm not
doing enough of something or concentrating on
the wrong thing in life? Like maybe being overly
worried about my penmanship? That's called obsessing over
something. Without a doubt, the psychiatrist pegged me: bipolar with OCD.

THE **DIAGNOSIS** WAS A **RELIEF.**

The diagnosis was a relief. I wouldn't say it was like coming to a finish line
in a marathon, because illness is endless work, but it was like running for a long time
and finally coming to a water station. I'm not done yet, but at least someone is giving
me a hand and I have time to take a breath.

What's, well, *crazy* about the whole thing is that even though I felt awful for years
and did enough research to get half of my diagnosis right, I never would have sought a
diagnosis on my own. It took a friend hauling me to the counseling center on campus,
when she had her own appointment, for me to understand that I didn't have the blues
or melodrama-itis but a diagnosable, treatable illness. I needed that diagnosis—any
diagnosis, as long as it explained how I was feeling—and it was vindicating. But it also
meant I couldn't shy away from reality anymore, and that was scary. Once you know
you have an illness, any kind of illness, it's challenging to ignore it. Even if you choose
not to do anything about it, you're now hyperaware of any behavior that you know
you shouldn't be engaging in or of any symptom that shows through. You can, even if
you would prefer not to, identify when you are doing something that is a hallmark or
symptom of the disease, and you realize you are a textbook case.

A diagnosis is an amazing thing. It's only the first step in many, because there's
medication and therapy and coping mechanisms to tease out, and that takes a long
time. But the peace that comes with having a term for what you experience—a term
that's not just "crazy" or "in your head" or "a complex"—is priceless. I never would

have known that I had an anxiety disorder if someone hadn't pointed it out to me. Thinking too much about everything was my norm; I was twenty-five before I realized that the way I think and focus and stare and obsess is not actually the way most other people act. My reality was what I assumed to be the reality of everyone.

Now that I know what I have and what it looks like, I have not only professionals who have my back but also the benefit of past experience to help me understand myself better. I can recognize when my moods are about to change, and I can plan for that. I can warn people I work with that if they interrupt me in the middle of something, even if it's a mundane task, I will not pay attention to what they're saying because I will be so caught up with finishing whatever it is I am doing—which is one reason I finish busywork much quicker than most people. I am engrossed with the repetitiveness of it all. I've discovered over the years that I should try not to start new television shows when I have work deadlines, because I don't have the ability to stop watching until I've finished all the available episodes. If I know I'm going to have a busy, socially exhausting day when I can use my mania to my advantage, I try to calendar downtime for the following day so that I can recharge and recuperate.

I spent at least ten years of my life feeling *off*. But in a simple diagnosis, plus a ton of work, trial and error with prescriptions, and introspection, I feel more powerful and in control of myself than I did my entire childhood and adolescence. I only wish someone had told me not that I was "crazy" but that I was sick, and there was a way to get better.

BEING HEARD AND HATING SOUND

by Stephanie Kuehn

When there are things about yourself you can't change—no matter how much you might want to and no matter how hard you try—it sort of throws your ideas about free will and agency into chaos. Not being able to control oneself is a far different experience than bumping up against outside obstacles that aren't in one's power to change. But our own thoughts, our feelings, our actions—those are the things that make up our internal existence and fundamentally define who we are. If we can't control what makes us *us*, what hope is there for finding agency anywhere else in our lives?

There are dark roads this kind of thinking can take you down, and sometimes the only escape from helplessness is hopelessness. But when it comes to beliefs about one's own character and self-concept, let me tell you, hopelessness is a pretty painful way to live. So while I'm not actually a hopeless person, or even a cynical one, it's taken me a long time to sort out my feelings and attitudes about the parts of myself I can't control.

When I was twelve, out of nowhere, I began growing irrationally and overwhelmingly angered by the most trivial thing: the sound of my father eating.

I love my dad dearly. I loved him then and I love him now. But he is a creature of strict habit, and when it comes to food, he can be counted on to eat pretty much the same thing every day. This meant, when I was living at home, that I had to hear him crunching away at Granny Smith apples and raw carrot sticks on a daily basis. And it's funny how the mind works: memories with emotion attached to them tend to be the strongest. Yet my recollection of such capstone events as losing my virginity or learning to drive are hazy at best. But after thirty years, I can still vividly picture my dad eating those damn apples—he'd down them in two bites. I can also recall my own emotional response, which was to silently seethe with fury and long for a way to wire my father's jaw shut.

My focus back then was on finding a way to control what my father did. I wanted him to stop eating those foods around me! But I failed wildly at all my efforts: dirty looks across the table, dramatic covering of my ears, hiding the offensive foods, even trying to eat them before he did or skipping meals in the passive-aggressive hope that he'd want me back at the table more than he wanted to eat the foods that annoyed me. What I really had no control over, of course, was the irrational sense of rage that bubbled up inside me whenever I was forced to endure these sounds that I loathed. In truth, I never quite know how to describe my reaction to sounds I don't like, other than use the phrase "instant homicidal fury." It sounds ridiculous, I realize, but that's why it's such a problem. The rage is like a light switch, and it's totally out of proportion with what's actually happening. The only way I can explain it is to ask you to imagine that the sound of someone eating evoked the same response in you as hearing fingernails being dragged across a chalkboard. The experience is painful—pain that tells you someone is hurting you—and the response is a reflex, not a choice. But when no one else experiences sound the way that you do . . . that means it's your problem.

As it turned out, trying to control my father was a useless endeavor anyway. It wasn't long before I was becoming enraged by my mother's gum chewing, then her best friend's mouth smacking and scratchy voice. This strange sensitivity of mine continued to grow and spread, to other people and other sounds, finally coalescing into a long list of triggers that torment me to this day: an assortment of noises made by other people's bodies that I cannot control and long to escape (a few visual triggers bother me as well). This list includes, but is not limited to: sniffling, slurping, swallowing, smacking, throat clearing, coughing, crunchy-food eating, blowing air through one's teeth, gum chewing, seeing someone chew gum, ice chewing, laptop tapping, phone tapping, certain voices, certain words—like "supper"—excessive fidgeting or body movement of any kind, dogs licking their paws excessively, people who go "Pah!"

after taking a sip of something hot, and finally, the sight of someone sucking on the end of a hoodie string.

Superweird, I get it. The problem is only made worse by the fact that there is something contextual about it. Certain people are more triggering than others, as are certain situations. It's about the sound . . . but it's also more than that.

Sometimes feeling terrible things makes you feel terrible about yourself, and that's what happened to me. I never told anyone about my weird sound fixation because I thought it made me out to be an awful person. No one else was bothered by these things, at least not to the extent I was. It was obvious that while these aren't sounds anybody loves—and they are ones that many people find annoying—my reaction to them was a real problem. It began to severely impact my daily functioning. I couldn't stand to be in a cubicle at work, or go to restaurants that served chips or other crunchy things. I couldn't sit in a movie theater or eat dinner at other people's homes—I couldn't stand the sound of my husband *brushing his teeth*. I am a social person by nature, but my first thought upon entering any social situation quickly became: *Is there a way I can escape if I need to?*

Compounding the problem was the subsequent loneliness. Or more accurately, the *aloneness* that I felt. I quickly found out that these aren't the kind of complaints or issues anyone wants to hear about. Understandably, people get defensive when told that the sounds they make are repulsive or intolerable. So I opted to do what anyone would do when they have a weird off-putting personal thing going on: I kept the whole thing inside me and wrote myself off as a controlling, bitchy kind of person.

It wasn't until maybe ten years ago, coinciding with the start of my graduate studies in psychology, that I stopped to consider what a mental illness really is. According to the American Psychiatric Association's *Diagnostic and Statistical Manual of Mental Disorders* (*DSM-5*), as referenced on page twenty of the 2013 edition, such an illness is characterized by both (1) "clinically significant disturbance in an individual's cognition, emotion regulation, or behavior" and (2) "distress or disability in social, occupational, or other important activities." That all felt familiar, and it occurred to me—for the first time—to sit down at a computer and research: "hates the sound of other people eating," which is how I discovered that . . . I really wasn't alone. Not at all! It turned out there were many,

I'M NO LONGER ALONE.

many other people in the world who had the same oddly wired brain that I did. These people described the exact same details about the development of their condition: onset during young adolescence, an initial fixation on one family member that eventually generalized to other people and other sounds; the very same triggers (repetitive eating, breathing, and related sounds); the very same emotional response of rage and violent impulses; and the very same awareness that the response was irrational, leading to a deep sense of personal shame over having such awful thoughts.

It also turned out that this condition has a name. A couple of them, really. It's known as either selective sound sensitivity syndrome (4S) or more commonly, misophonia, meaning "hatred of sound." Unfortunately, merely learning about misophonia has done nothing to fix the actual problem—I've found no solution to the symptoms. Yet despite the lack of resolution, this knowledge has still managed to deeply change me. I'm no longer alone, and that very fact has altered the way I see myself. It's helped me appreciate the power of validation, of knowing that how I exist in the world is an experience shared by others. It means my misophonia is something I can externalize. It's something I deal with, yes, but it's not a defect in character or a symptom of moral failing. It's not *me*. This distinction matters. A lot.

Being able to contextualize my misophonia in a healthy way has undoubtedly altered my beliefs, not just about myself but about others, as well. For all its unpleasantness, living with sound sensitivity has afforded me a heightened awareness of the impact my actions have on others. It's pushed me to try to validate the internal experiences of those around me, and to not shy away or avoid those truths that might cause them to feel vulnerable or shameful. By choosing a career in the mental health field, I'm striving to put some of my sensitivity back into my environment in a way that's constructive and meaningful and aligned with my values.

That isn't to say I don't continue to struggle. I do. Every day. My ability to change my environment with regard to trigger sounds is fairly restricted. Unlike people who are sensitive to scents, for example, there's no culturally accepted means for announcing that one is sensitive to sounds and to ask others to control their bodies accordingly in deference to my comfort and needs.

Perhaps that might change someday as misophonia becomes more well-known, although I don't know that I'd like that. Having the space to acknowledge that my misophonia is real is probably enough. For a condition that is defined by a desire to control the uncontrollable, any expectation of increased control is likely to cause more frustration. You can't *really* control other people, and for me, at least, it's healthier to try to accept that reality. Acceptance, I've come to believe, is an act of free will. An expression of my personal agency.

And in the end, if acceptance fails to materialize, there's no danger I'll ever actually act on my rageful impulses. I happen to be a fan of pragmatism. That means wherever I go, no matter where I am, you can be sure I'll always be carrying a pair of earplugs with me.

Just in case.

I HATE TO INTERRUPT THIS CONVERSATION ABOUT MENTAL ILLNESS, BUT GUESS WHAT—I'M AUTISTIC

by Mike Jung

On the first day of fourth grade, just a few weeks after my family had moved from California to New Jersey, I walked into the cafeteria at my new school for the first time, and it was like nothing I'd ever experienced before. It was as if I'd materialized inside a violent ocean of noise, an almost-intelligible mix of sharp, staccato words overlaid with a shapeless, droning buzz. At the same time, my visual perception grew foggy and remote. It was as if everything in the room had receded several feet into the distance, even though I was completely motionless. In retrospect, it's clear how many levels of comprehensive newness I was facing—*everything* was new: the room, the building, the school system, the way people talked and dressed and moved and looked, not to mention every face in sight. But at the time, most of that affected me subconsciously. The impressions I was most conscious of were defined by sight and sound.

I didn't have any understanding of things like sensory processing difficulties or auditory hypersensitivity at that time. But despite my ignorance, I was experiencing them, as I have every day of my life. I lacked the self-awareness to realize how far over the edge that first moment in the cafeteria had propelled me. I didn't have the slightest inkling that I might be autistic, of course. Very few people did: the 1970s were anything but a golden era of enlightenment regarding neurodiversity.

I was and am autistic. I was diagnosed in August 2016, and I started telling a select group of people about it not long after. The initial responses ranged from "I adore you" to "I'm so honored that you're telling me" to "Oh, I knew you were autistic from the moment we first met." But I'm happy to say that my early confidantes unanimously responded to my disclosure in a spirit of celebratory support. That was exactly what I needed. Of equal importance were the things these friends and colleagues didn't say, like "I'm so sorry," "Are you okay?," "I don't think you're autistic," or other ableist, neurotypically centered statements.

It's not like that collectively positive response happened by accident. It wasn't as though I'd hired a plane to randomly drop flyers with my diagnosis printed on them. I told people I trust, naturally. I've become friends with some thoroughly wonderful people since beginning my career as a children's author, which means the number of individuals who qualify for the "Trusted by Mike" designation had gone way up in recent years.

Autism is still profoundly misunderstood and demonized in our society, and we know from long, hard, and lamentably current experience that bigotry doesn't need to be visible to remain viable. Even so, sharing this essential new understanding of myself wasn't an act I planned to limit to friends and family. I'm a children's author with multiple books on the shelves, and I've spent the past few years being relatively loudmouthed on the topics of race and neurodiversity. I didn't pursue either of those subjects knowing they'd help prepare me to go public with the fact that I'm autistic, but they did. If I'd been diagnosed ten years ago, I'd definitely have been frightened to tell anyone, because I've internalized as much antiautistic stigma as the next person. But I now understand how healing it is to shed all those layers of confusion and misinformation. I now know the value of unashamedly telling the world exactly who I am, and that's exactly what I've been doing.

It's exciting, unsettling, and, by now, expected—I've actually been having conversations about autism with Miranda (I'm her husband) for years. Pro tip: it's very helpful being married to someone who understands things about you that you maybe don't entirely understand on your own. I still needed to digest this whopping slice of new self-knowledge, of course—that revealing oneself can be powerful—because we always must do that as part of the process of discovery. And make no mistake: doing so has been enormously positive for me.

I discovered there's also a huge amount of relief, because after almost half a century of existence, I finally have an explanation for *so many things*! That moment in the cafeteria was so horrible because I'm autistic and have auditory processing difficulties! I get very, very absorbed in projects because I'm autistic and often hyperfocus on things that interest me! That random adult who told me in seventh grade that I'm "like a cartoon character" said it because I'm autistic and was teaching myself social behaviors through trial and error! It was also because he was a thundering asshole!

It hasn't been all shits and grins, of course. That "teaching myself social behaviors" thing, for example, was a window into my entire childhood, adolescence, and early adulthood. There were things I needed to learn differently from most of the people around me, and the amount of useful, appropriate support I received back then was exactly zero. At the same time, the criticism I received felt infinite, especially when I tried to articulate my struggles. A person who I probably shouldn't have been friends with once told me I needed to stop "thinking things through" in social situations and just "let my instincts take over." In retrospect, I wish I'd replied, "What the hell are you *talking* about, 'let my instincts take over'?" He might as well have said, "Just try really hard to grow a third arm between your shoulder blades and eventually it'll happen!" Nothing about those situations felt instinctive; I had to learn how to navigate them in other ways.

I did, eventually, to the point where people now sometimes describe me as outgoing, friendly, and socially skilled. It's quite a change from the days when I'd get those "Dude, stop thinking things through" comments, which I took at face value for so long. These days, I better understand what those comments really meant, but that understanding still feels new. Whether or not the speaker in question was conscious of it, he was really saying, "You're doing it wrong. There's one right way to do this—your way is wrong. There's one right way to *exist*—your existence is wrong." Because I'm extraordinarily skilled at internalizing casual toxicity, I bought that perspective. I spent a very long time—including more than a decade during which I contemplated suicide daily—believing there was an infinite number of things wrong with me. But there isn't, and that just might be the way in which my autism diagnosis gave me the most relief, signaling: *There's an explanation.* There's nothing wrong *with me.*

There's nothing wrong with the fact that I limit how much time I spend in restaurants that quickly overwhelm me with loud acoustics. There's nothing wrong with never being interested in vapid small talk and always being interested in meaningful soul talk. There's nothing wrong with engaging in stimming behaviors like cracking my shoulder. I know it gives some people the creeps, but come on—I'm not cracking *anyone else's* shoulder. There's nothing wrong with being the kid who skips out on playing Marco Polo in the swimming pool in favor of retreating to an unoccupied room and reading an Anne McCaffrey novel, as I often did at my cousins' house in the Hollywood Hills.

It's very healing to have that realization, but of course it's not really as simple as saying, "Yo, there's nothing wrong with yours truly." After spending most of my life internalizing the idea that *everything* was wrong with me, I wasn't able to just flip a switch and go from "I'm a piece of shit" to "I'm okay and fuck you if you think I'm not!" Memories are powerful, and my back file of overwhelmed and/or humiliated moments is enormous. That cafeteria moment in fourth grade. The time when what felt like an entire locker room of seventh and eighth graders cornered and threatened me while the phys ed teacher sat and watched through an office window. The night in high school when my own brother asked me to stay in my room while his friends came over, then barked, "Get a social life!" when I refused. That graduation party during college when I was so stricken by social anxiety that I sat, unspeaking, in a chair for an hour before I could make myself get up and leave. And on, and on, and on.

Those memories have permanent residency in my psyche. Most of them have satellite memories, too, because unlike the characters I write about, I wasn't strong, resilient, or easily inclined to stand up for myself. Too many of those memories of mistreatment are accompanied by memories of how I just took the mistreatment, then went into a psychic tailspin.

It took me a very long time to teach myself how to cope with those memories and feelings in a healthy way, and until I did, my coping mechanisms were catastrophically unhealthy. I wasn't conscious of being autistic or how society treats autistic people, but I was very conscious of how overwhelming and disorienting it felt to be alive. A couple of years ago, I told a therapist (a pretty good one) about how chaotic and limitless the thoughts in my head have always felt. He tried to frame my perspective with a metaphor: Imagine our thoughts are individually contained in boxes with lids on them, and that most people can pick which box they want to open, thereby releasing that thought. Is it like all the boxes in your mind are always open? I said not really—it's more like all the boxes are open, launching themselves into the air, and aggressively hurling their contents into my face over and over. I tried to mute the psychic onslaught through alcohol, drugs, and escapist entertainment, because when I didn't, I mostly felt despair.

Good times! Hashtag irony. When the world we've constructed as human beings is actively hostile to those of us who are autistic, good times can be hard to come by. The world has always felt like an alien landscape to me in some ways, and while I've learned to navigate it on neurotypical terms, the cost to my mental health has been higher than anyone should have to face. Autism is not mental illness, but attempted compliance with nonautistic standards of behavior have played a central role in my lifelong battles with depression and anxiety.

I did my best to teach myself how to meet those deeply biased standards, with some success. I acquired neurotypical social skills through observation, practice, (very painful) trial and error, and brow-wrinkling thought processes. And I always knew the emotions I had such difficulty expressing back then were real, even when society as a whole took every opportunity to tell me how undesirable and harmful my way of existing was. But I didn't know any other way to express those feelings. I didn't have the self-knowledge I needed to feel whole, and to truly comprehend why all the messages of unworthiness I'd internalized were completely wrong. I also didn't have friends, artists, and advocates in my life to learn from, and communities to immerse myself in. And more to the point, I didn't have the language, communication skills, and conviction I needed to push back; I needed more coping mechanisms.

Well, after all those years of isolation and self-loathing, my diagnosis has given me an incredible new coping mechanism. That's underselling the diagnosis, in fact. I'm finally entering a period of intense self-education about autistic history, culture, and especially activism. I think about noncompliance with a society that persists in minimizing the value of autistic lives. I think about the idea I've been kicking around for a book with an autistic protagonist, how important that idea now feels, and how stunningly good it'll be if I can pull it off. Knowledge is power, and self-knowledge is the best knowledge. I feel powerful. It's a strange and wonderful feeling.

I'm not going to stop telling the world that I'm autistic. Organizations like Autism Speaks continue to repudiate the importance of autistic voices, but they won't stop me. There are still too many damaging portrayals of autism in popular culture, including in books, and I intend to open an industrial-sized barrel of elbow grease to apply in that area—I mean, of course. I *am* a children's author, after all. As I learn more about the history of autism and autism advocacy, I understand more about what a long and tiring road lies ahead, but I intend to follow the many stellar people who've been on that road for much longer than me.

Oh hey, here's another great thing about knowing I'm autistic: I know some of those stellar people I just mentioned, and *I get to talk to them about this stuff*! I'm walking into the autistic community as a neon-green newbie, and being able to talk with and learn from such superb people is wonderful. The fact that some of those people are friends and colleagues in the world of children's and YA literature only makes it that much better, and the generosity of friends like Corinne Duyvis and Marieke Nijkamp has helped me begin expanding my circle of like-minded souls beyond the world of kidlit.

There's also Miranda (I'm married to her, remember). She drew a trail between several different books about autism that eventually led to Nick Walker, who's a significant voice in the world of autistic activism. If I'm not mistaken, he's also the only autistic aikido instructor in the country, if not the world. Nick is the cofounder and lead teacher of Aikido Shusekai, a remarkable martial arts dojo in Berkeley that's a twenty-minute drive from my home.

I mean, come on—it's like the universe was shouting, "DUDE, CARPE DIEM!" at me through a cosmic megaphone. It took some time, but I finally clawed through a lifetime of anxiety and shame about my athletic incompetence to become a student at Shusekai. In so doing, I discovered how badly I needed a community that unstintingly embraces neurological differences. Nick and cofounder Azzia Walker (who identifies as neurodivergent, and who Nick is married to) have created such a community. Their progressive views on neurodiversity and compassion-infused aikido teachings are healing on a level that's completely new to me. The exhausting effort to conform to neurotypical norms had always felt mandated by society, but now? Now I have a place where that effort is completely unnecessary. I've never felt so free of judgment. I've never felt so *seen*.

This is my life now, and I can hardly believe my good fortune. When Miranda tells me how great it is to see me "melting," I know she's talking about my current (and lifelong) process of shedding endless layers of physical and psychological tension. The knowledge that I'm autistic has made it possible for me to start stripping away those layers, and to fully realize that my presence in this world is, in fact, a good thing. When someone tells me how genuine and heartfelt I am on Facebook, I understand that the truly meaningful part of what they're saying is not about my skill at using Facebook but about the genuine and heartfelt emotion that I'm expressing. When a close friend says they adore me, it's because they know I genuinely adore them in return. When someone says I make them laugh with my sense of humor, it's no accident—I *am* pretty damned funny. I also have a tremendous singing voice, a very friendly cat, and excellent taste in doughnuts.

So don't call me crazy, because conflating autism with insanity is factually wrong. Don't call me a burden, a tragedy, or an inspiration, either. Don't call me a liar—I'm not making any of this up, and I've spent most of my life trying to figure myself out, which I guarantee is longer than you've spent trying to figure *me* out. Do not under any circumstance call me *curable*, because autism isn't a disease in need of a cure—it's an essential and inextricable part of who I am as a human being. If someone believes, impossibly, that curing me of autism is desirable, that person also believes that my existence as the person I truly am is *not* desirable. You understand how that might make someone want to start flipping tables, right?

There are plenty of other things you're welcome to call me, though. Call me a husband and father. Call me someone who tries to be a good friend. Call me a children's author and a future librarian. Call me disabled. Call me neurodivergent. Call me human. I am, you know. I may be different in some ways from nonautistic people, but I'm different in some ways from every other autistic person, too, and whatever those differences may be, I'm 100 percent human.

Call me autistic.

Don't call me Mikey, though. I hate that.

AUTISTIC AUTHORS

WHO MIKE JUNG THINKS ARE GREAT by Mike Jung

- **CORINNE DUYVIS!** Author of *Otherbound*, *On the Edge of Gone*, and *Guardians of the Galaxy: Collect Them All*; cofounder of Disability in Kidlit. corinneduyvis.net

- **LYN MILLER-LACHMANN!** Author of *Gringolandia*, *Rogue*, and *Surviving Santiago*; editor of short story anthology *Once Upon a Cuento*; translator of multiple books, including *O Mundo Segundo* (*The World in a Second*), and *O Mundo Dá Muitas Voltas* (*Three Balls of Wool*). lynmillerlachmann.com/category/blog

- **MARIEKE NIJKAMP!** Author of the *New York Times* #1 bestseller *This Is Where It Ends* and *Before I Let Go*; founding member of We Need Diverse Books. mariekenijkamp.com/musings

- **SALLY J. PLA!** Author of *The Someday Birds*, *Stanley Will Probably Be Fine*, and *Benji, the Bad Day, and Me*. sallyjpla.com

- **NICK WALKER!** Coauthor of the webcomic *Weird Luck*; essayist, memoirist, and author published in numerous anthologies, including *The Real Experts: Readings for Parents of Autistic Children* and *Loud Hands: Autistic People, Speaking*; cofounder of indie publisher Autonomous Press. neurocosmopolitanism.com

CHAPTER TWO

WHERE "CRAZY" MEETS CULTURE

WE SEE mental illness portrayed in popular culture all the time, whether or not we're aware of it. Sometimes it's at the center of the story, and sometimes it's on the sidelines. There are times when mental illness is well rendered, but there are also times when it is portrayed in disturbing and/or damaging ways. In either case, as well as the many cases in between, popular culture can be a window into mental illness. It can also serve as a mirror, in which those who do struggle with their mental health may finally see pieces of themselves and their experiences reflected.

Of course, it's not only in *popular* culture that we find depictions of and beliefs surrounding mental health. It exists in all facets of culture: our family, our friends, our heritage, our education, and every other piece of the story that makes us who we are.

From representations of hysteria in horror movies to the unrealistic depiction of women in music and television, and from intergenerational pain to the aftermath of a school shooting, the conversation surrounding mental health in culture and pop culture is wide and varied—and crucial for continuing the dialogue about mental health.

THE DEVIL INSIDE

by Christine Heppermann

To call me a timid child would be putting it mildly. I was the scarediest of scaredy-cats. I was a thumb-sucking ball of irrational fears in a smock dress. My most vivid childhood memories involve running away from things. I ran panicked down the sidewalk because, no matter how hard my parents worked to convince me that Frizzy, the neighbors' elderly schnauzer, wanted only to play, to me his wagging tail signaled a savage desire to leap the chain-link fence and chew my face off. I sprinted through the crosswalk at school every day, crying, because I refused to believe the cars would stop. They were so big and powerful. I was so small. Clearly a few measly crossing guards—kids, just like me—could never prevent a bloodthirsty Oldsmobile from mowing me down.

I usually fled the TV room during commercials for scary movies, but something about the ad for *The Exorcist* intrigued me. I don't remember much about it except for a few relatively benign images—fog, shadowy figures under a lamppost, a looming house, tinkly theme music. That was enough to send me running, but not too far. I stood in the hallway, right outside the door, and listened.

That summer, during a visit with relatives in Missouri, I learned that my aunt and her boyfriend had seen *The Exorcist*. I *begged* her to tell me about it. Because she didn't want me crawling into bed with her every night, too scared to sleep on my own, she said no.

"Pleasepleasepleasepleasepleasepleasepleasepleasepleaseplease?" (For a timid child, I could be incredibly persistent.)

Finally, probably to get me to leave her alone, she relented and gave me a basic recap.

Big mistake.

There's no running away from the devil, especially if he is inside you.

I spent the next, oh, seven or eight years in near constant terror, convinced that, like Regan, the girl in the movie, I would be possessed. How could I possibly escape such a fate? I needed to remain vigilant, to stay awake—literally and figuratively—and keep Satan out.

It's not hard to see why this phobia took hold and refused to let go. I was Catholic. I attended Catholic school. I went to Mass with my family every Sunday and on holy days of obligation. To me the devil wasn't just a fake movie monster, like Freddy Krueger and Chucky. Satan was real, and, according to the Church, his sole reason for existing was to mess with people's heads—to trick them into doing Bad Things.

A case in point: in 1977, the news broke that the recently apprehended "Son of Sam" serial murderer David Berkowitz blamed his crimes on a demonically possessed black Labrador retriever that ordered him to kill. Most people, I assume, thought, *Wow, what a nut.* Me? Let's just say my suspicions about Frizzy took on a whole new dimension.

My fear peaked the year I turned twelve, the same age as Regan, whose increasingly disturbing behavior prompts her frantic mother to call in the priests. In addition to the typical middle school activities of scanning one's chin for pimples and pubic area for sprouting hairs, I steeled myself for other, even more disturbing changes. Would I sear my flesh with holy water? Scream profanities in math class? Turn to guard an opponent during a soccer game and rotate my head 180 degrees? I still hadn't seen *The Exorcist*, but, contrary to my own self-interest, had found out more about it. (Not from my aunt! She had learned her lesson.) I didn't enjoy torturing myself by obsessing over every gruesome detail . . . Or did I? Maybe I did, because, it seemed, I couldn't stop.

My religious faith both reassured me and made everything worse. Supposedly, it protected me against evil, but, in my understanding, it also taped a big fat "Come and Get Her" sign to my back. If Satan wanted nothing more than to corrupt believers and lead them to damnation, then I was Satan bait. I fretted over every "sin," no matter how small, sure that even the narrowest crack in my virtue gave the devil an entrance. But I couldn't seem to stop sinning. I'd go to confession, obtain absolution from the priest, and then tap-dance right back to the edge of the fiery pit. I'd play with a Ouija board at sleepovers—that's how the demon Pazuzu, aka Captain Howdy, begins communicating with Regan—and then spend the rest of the night lying petrified in my sleeping bag, pleading with God for forgiveness.

Once, when I was walking back to my classroom after an all-school Mass, Sister Alice, the principal, pulled me out of line. She dragged me down to her office and confronted me about the novelty comb sticking out of my back pocket. On the comb's long yellow handle, red bubble letters spelled out the words "Cheap Thrill." I had bought it as a joke from the cheesy mall store Spencer's Gifts, but Sister Alice didn't see the humor. I remember her face, red with fury, as she screamed at me for daring to bring something so vulgar and disrespectful into church. Had I no shame? Well, it turns out, I did: I burst into tears and later prayed—and prayed and prayed and prayed—that Satan hadn't noticed all the commotion and marked me down for a house call.

Flash forward to now: I'm not a practicing Catholic. There are things I really miss about the religion, such as the rituals that filled me with awe and the sense of belonging to a supportive community united by shared beliefs. But, ultimately, the cycle of fear and guilt wore me down. I realize that not all Catholics berate and second-guess themselves quite as, um, intensely as I did. But looking back now at my fearful childhood self, I see her as trapped in a pattern that exists not only in the Church but in the culture at large, a pattern that encourages girls and women to view themselves as, if not the devil, then certainly members of his team.

Back in middle school, along with my taboo comb, I had a T-shirt, also purchased at the mall and without my parents' knowledge, emblazoned with "Good Girls Go to Heaven, But Bad Girls Go Everywhere." Sometimes I wore it secretly under my school-uniform blouse, like a superhero concealing her true identity beneath a bland veneer. I liked my comb; I liked my T-shirt; I liked the (mild) sense of freedom and exploration they represented—but I knew I wasn't supposed to. To avoid reproach, I learned how to pose as a Good Girl, but even that persona couldn't completely shield me. It seemed that, for girls, there was no such thing as "good" enough.

The example of Sister Alice notwithstanding, the Catholic Church gives women little power. It has no place for women in its official hierarchy. Bishops make all the rules, and guess what? Bishops are men. Celibate men, for the most part. Men who, over the centuries, have had much to say about women's minds and women's bodies and what women should and should not do with them. Now I find it ironic that I spent so many years with a fear of being possessed by Satan, when, all that time, without realizing it, I was already being controlled.

> FOR **GIRLS**, THERE WAS NO SUCH THING AS **"GOOD"** ENOUGH.

Leaving the Church didn't give me an automatic "Get Out of The Patriarchy Free" card. Obviously, *The Exorcist* didn't reflect just upon Catholicism. It was part of pop culture, and its portrayal of evil as a girl on the cusp of turning, physically, into a woman seemed—and continues to seem—all too familiar. *Help me*, Regan manages to scrawl on the skin of her stomach for Father Damien to read. In other words: *Save me from myself. Rescue the Good Girl from the Bad Girl within.*

In 1968, the year I was born, Hollywood produced the mother of all devil-inside horror movies, *Rosemary's Baby*, based on the popular novel by Ira Levin. Rosemary, played by Mia Farrow, is pregnant and worries that something is horribly wrong, either with her or the baby or both of them. It turns out that she's right, but she doesn't discover the full truth of her situation until days after giving birth, when she sees her son for the first time and stares into his glowing yellow eyes.

Lucky for me, I somehow avoided *Rosemary's Baby* as a kid. Otherwise, it would surely have added vivid new rooms to my mental chamber of torture as I imagined myself, for instance, slurping down raw chicken hearts and rocking a black bassinet beneath an upside-down crucifix.

I also would have been too young to grasp what makes Rosemary's story chilling to the core. Forget the spooky tropes. What keeps me up at night now is thinking about how the state of women's rights, fifty years after the movie's release, is still so precarious. Isn't that the real evil? That after decades of what we'd thought was feminist progress, the image of a woman manipulated into giving up control of her own body, her own desires, seems routine.

Who really preys upon Rosemary? Satan rapes her, but only after her husband, her doctor, and others create the conditions for that to happen. They're secretly using her while pretending to have her best interests at heart. What *she* wants, what *she* feels, doesn't matter to them. And when she begins to voice suspicions, they shoot them down. They tell her over and over that she doesn't know what's good for her— *they* do.

If you're really in the mood for a scare, watch the scene in which Rosemary wakes up groggy and confused after the rape and turns to her husband, Guy, for answers. Guy is a struggling actor who's sick of struggling. Does he fire his agent, maybe take classes to improve his craft? Nope! He offers his wife's womb to a satanic cult, without her knowledge, in exchange for career success. To cover up what he's done, he lies—and lies and lies. When Rosemary asks him about the scratch marks on her chest and the bruises on her thighs, he tells her that she drank too much the night before and passed out. (The second part of his explanation is true—he drugged her dessert.) But, he says, he had sex with her anyway because that's what she wanted, right? Because she wants a baby, and, he claims, he wants one, too. About the sex they supposedly had, he jokes, "It was kinda fun in a necrophile sort of way." And even though Rosemary still feels uneasy, she lets him convince her that he did what he did—what he *says* he did—out of love. That if she has any misgivings about what happened to her body, she's overreacting.

Now consider another classic movie about a husband messing with his wife's mind. In the 1944 American film *Gaslight*, a man doesn't want his wife to find out that he's a murderous jewel thief. So he orchestrates an elaborate scheme to trick her into believing that she's going insane. The film's title has become a term for a form of psychological abuse. To "gaslight" someone is to manipulate her into questioning her sanity—as if to signal, "I'm not the one with the problem, honey—it's you! I'm in the right, you're in the wrong."

Guy tries to gaslight Rosemary into believing that everything is fine, that she's crazy if she thinks otherwise. In constant stabbing pain during the early months of her pregnancy, she finally breaks down sobbing to female friends. They surround her, comfort her, denounce her obstetrician for dismissing her suffering as normal. They urge her to see a different doctor as soon as possible. In that fleeting moment, with the support of other women, Rosemary has clarity. She has power. Something is indeed very wrong, and she is determined to fix it. But when she tells Guy that she's going to seek a second opinion, he gaslights her yet again. He calls her friends "a bunch of not-very-bright bitches." He's basically saying, "They're the Bad Girls who shouldn't be trusted. Keep them out of your business, out of the room, out of power, under control. Don't let them lead you astray."

I haven't quite figured out whether it's a case of life imitating art or the other way around that Roman Polanski, the director of *Rosemary's Baby*, was arrested in 1977 on charges of drugging and raping a thirteen-year-old model he was photographing for a magazine. The tactics of Polanski's defenders—and there were, and are, many, especially in the entertainment industry—could have come straight from Guy's playbook: claim the victim wanted it, despite her insistence that she repeatedly begged Polanski to stop and take her home; blame the girl's mother for allowing her to go with him, as if, instead of sending her daughter out on a modeling job under adult supervision, she had sold her into prostitution. Polanski eventually pled guilty to the charge of unlawful sex with a minor (statutory rape), but he fled the country before sentencing and has since lived in Europe, where he continues to make movies. In 2002, he won an Academy Award for Best Director for *The Pianist*.

"You were crazy. You were really ka-pow out of your mind," Guy tells Rosemary after she tries but fails to run away. Well, thanks for sharing, dude, but that's just not true. As Guy's actions demonstrate, there are things in the world that women should fear. Maybe Frizzy was a sweetheart, but some dogs *do* bite. Some men in power strive to deny women basic health care, equality in the workplace, and reproductive rights. Some men follow us home, or slip things into our drinks, or ask us over to "talk business." Afterward, they try to convince us that what they did to our bodies wasn't a crime because we "wanted it"; otherwise, why would we have worn that dress/had that drink/accepted the invitation? They force-feed us lies about ourselves until it seems we have no choice but to swallow them.

Pretending to be a good, obedient girl, Rosemary lies quietly in bed while Guy feeds her his explanation. And then, after he leaves—when the moment feels right—she gets up and walks down the hall. She opens the door and enters the room where her captors have gathered. No longer will she let them possess her. They can jabber on all day long, telling her she's wrong or bad or out of her mind, but she won't listen. Finally, she's not afraid. She knows what she knows.

These days, when fear or doubt or shame starts to creep in, I resist the impulse to run. I try to have faith in myself and stand my ground. I think about what singer-songwriter Florence Welch of the band Florence and the Machine says about dancing with the devil on your back—it's too hard. So you know what you have to do, right?

Shake him off.

10 HORROR FILMS ABOUT FEAR

by Stephanie Kuehn

- **ARACHNOPHOBIA**
  (fear of spiders)

- **THE BIRDS**
  (fear of birds)

- **THE CRUSH**
  (fear of a teenage girl)

- **FINAL DESTINATION**
  (fear of flying)

- **PONTYPOOL**
  (fear of language)

- **THE RING**
  (fear of losing someone
  you love)

- **THE STEPFORD WIVES**
  (fear of women)

- **THE VANISHING**
  (fear of tight spaces)

- **VERTIGO**
  (fear of heights)

- **THE VILLAGE**
  (fear of reality)

MANIC ~~PIXIE DREAM~~ GIRL

by S. Jae-Jones

I do not exist; I am a fantasy.

The first time I heard someone tell me so, I was smoking clove cigarettes out the third-floor window of my dorm in New York City's Chinatown. A friend from my American Literature course was sitting in my room, ostensibly there to "study," although I suspected otherwise. What was the point in "studying" for a literature class anyway? We would be graded on essays, not exams. *Perhaps I'm being ungenerous*, I thought, flicking ash onto the cockroach-ridden concrete streets below. Perhaps my friend really was there to work.

"Focus," he said.

We were making our way through the Puritans, or rather, my friend was doing his best to engage me in discussion. He read the assigned reading aloud, asking questions, trying to get me to work. I was staring at the facade of the industrial building across the street, past which I could glimpse bits of a sparkling Manhattan through the broken-toothed smile of a jagged skyline.

"Focus," he said again as I stuck my head out the window for a better view. I knew, based on the angle at which he sat, that I wasn't the only one getting a better view. I knew and was ambivalent, more interested in his reaction than my own feelings.

"I'm listening," I replied.

But I wasn't. Not to his words, at any rate. I was listening to his tone of voice, to his silences, to the slight, self-conscious pauses in his speech. I couldn't have cared less about predestination or sin in early colonial American poetry. I was an indifferent student at best, one of those disgusting people who had the trick of obtaining good grades with minimal effort. What I *was* interested in was provoking a reaction. What I wasn't sure of was what I wanted that reaction to be.

"JJ!" he said sharply, jumping to his feet as I leaned farther out the window, dropping the rest of my cigarette and watching its glowing butt tumble like a firefly down to the gutter.

I grinned.

My friend grabbed me by the hand and pulled me back into the relative safety of my bedroom, wrapping one arm about my waist and guiding me gently to my bed. Now that I had provoked him, I wasn't so sure I liked the result. I had liked the idea of his concern in the abstract, but the concrete reality of his hand still pressing against my side made my skin crawl. I twisted out of his grip, twirling away with a laugh to hide my discomfort.

"You're impossible," he said.

"One can't believe in impossible things," I said, paraphrasing *Alice's Adventures in Wonderland*. "But then again, sometimes I've believed as many as six impossible things before breakfast."

The reference was lost on my friend, for all that he claimed to love children's literature as much as I did.

"You're so . . . mysterious," he said. "I can't figure you out." Despite my nimble sidesteps, he had managed to draw close again, and this time, I was definitely sure I didn't like it.

"I say what I mean and mean what I say." I was referencing *Alice* again, even though I knew my friend wouldn't get it. Because I knew he wouldn't get it.

"I don't know." He shook his head. "I've never met anyone like you. I didn't think girls like you existed."

"What, like I'm a fantasy?" I laughed again, but he did not gainsay me. Instead, his face brightened, as though I had passed him the answer to a particularly difficult riddle. As though he agreed.

"You're impossible," he repeated, but this time it did not sound like censure or a rebuke on his lips. It sounded like a night full of stars, like disbelief and delight reflected in warm brown eyes. It sounded like awe.

Nineteen was my annus horribilis, the year I fell a thousand feet during a skiing accident and obliterated my left knee. At the time, the accident felt like a culmination of everything wrong that was happening to me, like snowflakes turning into a blizzard. I never knew which flake it was that set off the avalanche, but sometimes I think my so-called friend's words were the beginning of a year of destruction and rebirth. It was the year I had to leave school to recover from surgery, the year I lost touch with my first and fastest college friends. It was the year I upended myself, and the year I understood just how literal the angel and the demon on my shoulders could be.

I had been diagnosed with depression, then anxiety, back in high school. After some rounds of tepid therapy and low-dosage medication, my conditions were declared manageable, and life returned to normal. Then, senior year, I discovered the black relief of self-sabotage, the catharsis of the abyss, the angry abandon of reckless arrogance, and the diagnosis of bipolar disorder.

Just an adjustment, I thought. *I've been through depression. I can make it through this.*

I thought I knew the demon on my shoulder. I thought I knew depression, only to discover it was in fact the angel.

Mania wasn't something I had considered dangerous. When I was younger, my periods of mania were often written off as the foibles of an "artistic personality," and when I was older, the endearing quirks of a manic pixie dream girl. Sanitized, de-emphasized, trivialized.

"I didn't think girls like you existed."

Girls like Alaska Young from *Looking for Alaska*, like Natalie Portman's character from *Garden State*, like Kirsten Dunst's from *Elizabethtown*—they exist in fictional spaces, not in real life. They can't exist beyond the page or screen because they are two-dimensional paper dolls, while we live in a three-dimensional world. Without an Everyman's emotional journey to prop them up, they simply flop, limp and useless, back into the drawer with all the other toys.

"I didn't think girls like you existed."

That sentiment would be a repeated refrain in my life, blasted from the chorus of basic cishet white dudes that seemed to follow me like backup singers on tour. I never understood what exactly about me was impossible. Perhaps it was because I was a Real Girl and not a paper doll. Perhaps it was because I was a jumbled up Rubik's Cube of a human, all my sides and interests and passions mixed up and without order. Or perhaps it was because my mania made me sparkling, erratic, unpredictable.

Mysterious.

Magical.

I liked the idea of being magical. It fit with the idea of being a fantasy. I liked looking at the world like it was an unfolding flower of possibility, the most amazing Instagram filter mental illness could make. I liked making people laugh, I liked surprising them with spontaneity, I liked seeing their eyes light up with delight—I liked it, I liked it, I liked it.

But mania didn't make me magical; it made me reckless. It made me capricious, contradictory, and cruel. It made me incoherent. It didn't just make me dangerous, it made me a danger—to my family, to my friends, to myself.

Nineteen was the year I discovered how it made me a danger.

In my moments of clarity, I look back on that seemingly perpetual summer and realize that I'm one of the lucky ones. I survived. I more than survived; I *thrived*. The lacquer provided by money, by outward respectability, by supportive parents all but guaranteed that horrific consequences slid off me like rainwater on glass. I had the luxury of *time*—provided by privilege and forbearance—to find my path toward recovery. To remission. To realization.

> MANIA DIDN'T MAKE ME MAGICAL; IT MADE ME **RECKLESS.**

I lived. In living, I came to understand what my backup choir of cishet white dudes never did: that girls like me didn't exist, because we rarely get help.

The manic pixie dream girl is tragic, but I am not. In truth, I'm pretty mundane. As a child, I was a Good Kid—self-disciplined, conscientious, rule-abiding. Good Kids often grow up to be Boring Adults, and I'm no exception. I did Girl Scouts, took piano lessons, AP classes. I went to college, graduated early, found a job. I pay my taxes and my bills on time. I've even paid off my student loans. I am a productive, functioning member of society. I have bipolar disorder. Those last two things are not mutually exclusive.

I don't know why these facts are so hard for others to reconcile.

"I have bipolar disorder," I say.

"But you don't seem like it," they reply. "You seem so *normal!*"

Sometimes I wonder if having a mental illness is supposed to be visible. Am I supposed to bear the scars—both physical and metaphorical—of my disorder like a flag, like a warning? Do I wear a sign about my neck that reads: Here Be a Real-Life Crazy Person—Tread Carefully? What do people expect of me, once they know?

Those who love me know that I am large and contain multitudes, as Walt Whitman once wrote. Others probe and mine my history, sifting through my personal stories in the hopes of hitting the mother lode of hidden tragedy.

"How did you do it?" they ask. "How did you get better?"

I didn't. I survive with it. I live with it. I thrive with it, thanks to a combination of medication, therapy, and a wonderful support network.

Mental illness is a part of me. Living with bipolar disorder is like being the Goldilocks of your own brain, always in search of the state of Just Right. Just Right is when I'm Me—generally sanguine, frivolous, whimsical, with a touch of grumpy old lady. When I'm manic, I'm Too Much Me. When I'm depressed, I'm Not Enough Me.

But isn't that true of everyone? Aren't we all in search of a state of Just Right in our lives? In our relationships, in our jobs, in our souls? For me, finding balance is more than juggling a career, love, family, and passions; it's juggling Me. Myself. Entire novels are written about the quotidian struggles of the Everyman, the ups and downs, the joys and sorrows. "Relatable," readers say. "Finding the epic in the mundane, the universal in the specific." Is my story not relatable? Or is it worth telling only if it's tragic?

Of all places, you would think that fiction would be the space where I could exist. I wrote myself into a book, yet it still doesn't seem like I'm a Real Girl. I'm without character development, emotionally disconnected, unrealistic. Or perhaps that's just my protagonist, Liesl.

Negative reviews never troubled me. Arrogance ebbs and fades with my mania, but I can still put it on like an old jacket out of season. I am a genius. I am Kanye. Like *My Beautiful Dark Twisted Fantasy*, my work is messy, but not a mess. The plot is non-existent, the pacing uneven, the rules of the world unexplained, but those criticisms are craft based, objective, impersonal.

My bipolar disorder is personal.

"Write what you know," the old saying goes. To which I say, "Bullshit." I don't know any Goblin Kings, I've never lived in eighteenth-century Bavaria, nor do I compose music, all of which my protagonist knows intimately. My adage is this: "Write what you know to be true." Write your lived experience into existence. Write your truth.

In *Wintersong*, I wrote the things I knew to be true. I knew my passion for Mozart. I knew how hard it was to accept that my art was not worthless but worthwhile. I knew mania, and I knew melancholy, but I knew how both infused my thoughts and my entire being most of all.

Would it have been easier to write Liesl's journey without my truth? Perhaps, but then again, perhaps not. I don't know how else to exist. I don't know how to extract my mental illness from my existence, from my experiences as a creator. My scattered, racing thoughts, my whiplash emotional turns, my periods of bleak deadness and crippling self-doubt . . . For some, these traits made Liesl an unbelievable heroine.

I am an unbelievable heroine. The reality of my existence in a fantastic setting is unrealistic.

Maybe it would have been simpler, then, to write my truth as a work of contemporary fiction. To give life to my bipolar disorder as a force to be reckoned with, the black hole that launches everyone around me into orbit. But mental illness wasn't the monster in my life that it seemed to be in the books I read. To me, these portrayals weren't fantastic, even if they sometimes seemed like fantasy. These books were not my reality. These characters were larger than life in ways that I am not: made noble or tragic by their suffering.

But I'm not noble. I'm not tragic. I don't suffer. I don't struggle with a mental illness monster; I *am* the motherfucking monster.

Mental illness isn't a metaphor, and I loathe allegory as mental illness. The Underground was never meant to be an allegory. Liesl never finds a map to the labyrinth of the Goblin King's domain, just as I never found the map to my moods. But maybe it became an allegory in the writing of it. In writing Liesl out of the darkness, I was writing myself into the light.

There is a Korean fairytale called "The Woodcutter and the Heavenly Maiden," in which an Everyman woodcutter tricks a daughter of heaven into becoming his wife by stealing her robes while she is bathing. Without her robes, she cannot fly and return to the sky, instead weighed down by her earthly responsibilities—a husband and three children. Like the Scottish selkie, once the heavenly maiden finds her robes—her second skin—she puts them on and floats away, one child under each arm and the third held tight between her knees. As a little girl, I had an illustrated version of this story, given to me in the hopes that I would learn to read my milk tongue as eagerly and easily as I had learned English.

The image of the heavenly maiden flying away, the tail of her sash in her husband's hands, stayed with me long after my Korean language skills withered to an embarrassment. She looked like a kite, silk robes billowing out like butterfly wings against the clouds, her long, thin sash the string that kept her from becoming lost.

The fairy tale continues with the woodcutter following his wife and children by returning to the bathing pool where he first stole her robes. Each full moon, the heavenly maidens lower a washtub into the pool, filling it with water. The woodcutter climbs inside and is drawn up to heaven, where he reunites with his wife and children—and they live happily ever after.

Until they don't.

Homesick and worried about his aging mother, the woodcutter begs for use of a flying magical horse from the Sky King, who grants it reluctantly. He stipulates that the woodcutter can no longer set foot on Earth, for then he would forever be barred from heaven.

Even as I child, I could guess how the story would end before I got there. The woodcutter does precisely what the Sky King warns him not to do: he treads upon the ground and is no longer able to fly above the clouds. A sad tale, but the image to which I keep returning is the kite-wife and the woodcutter holding her string. For me, the story always ended here. I did not like to turn the page to get to its tragic ending, and instead preferred to imagine the maiden suspended forever between heaven and earth, free but safe.

Those who have flown kites understand the give-and-take between your will and the will of the winds. Those who have known me accept that they do not guide the kite, for I fly where the winds take me. The ones who hold my string keep me safe, but free. We dance, a delicate balance that is both holding on and letting go.

I have needed that string, that tether, to know that I matter. Matter. Mass. I have weight and depth and dimension. I have significance, for I am a human being, entire.

"You're impossible," he said, and I hope that this time, this recollection, I would tell my friend he is wrong.

But that's not what happened.

What happened was that in the moment I realized our friendship was fake, he decided our relationship was real. He sent me mixed CDs filled with songs about magical, mysterious girls, cobbling together an image of me built from the lyrics of Weezer's "El Scorcho" and "Stephanie Says" by the Velvet Underground.

His belief made me disappear.

So I ghosted him; I became a ghost. I left him with nothing but a concept: a manic pixie dream girl, there and gone in a flash.

I was real enough on my own.

CONSTELLATIONS OF SCARS

by Monique Bedard (Aura)

The dots were disconnected and they never made any sense, but the Constellations of Scars mapped all over my body tells my story

| multiple stories.

"Do your forgiveness work," she says. Even when I am lying lifeless and limp, with too many thoughts at the top of my head. They collect along the ceiling of my mind like helium balloons with nowhere to go, waiting to burst or deflate. I unlatch the skylight to release them to Creation and let them go to rest so we may all have peace.

There is no calm before the storm as lateral love is continually torn, right from my heart that's meant to be safe inside my chest, but they turn that love into hate that spreads viscously across their bodies and their faces. This is what holds me back from going home and connecting to what my spirit needs to know

| Longhouse.

There is so much to learn as I mourn the loss of knowledge and language and story.
It is through the pain of re | moval
dis | connection
dis | enfranchisement

                              and de | nial
                  that I am diss | ed and
                            dis | missed again, and again.

Gravel digs into my knees as I am begging to be heard, pleading to be seen, asking to be recognized, clawing tirelessly at the multiple layers of these identities.

I turn to my past to see a little girl who is lost and knows nothing but the screams and the pain of her innocence being ripped from her spirit, knowing that her story is about to change. When she looks further down the road, she can see her grandmother lying flat amongst the grass

| alone.

It was not her fault that her children were ripped straight from her arms as they disappeared into the dusty gray cloud of the unknown. She reflects on being a lost little girl as her parents were forced to sign those papers that robbed the family of all that they knew. They were no longer allowed to be Indigenous to this land. Who they are was erased from their story and replaced with a dollar sign and a single piece of land cut straight from the earth and placed within her hands. As dirt falls between the cracks of her fingers, she can feel the pain of being severed from her own identity. They are the only ones who know the land just like the back of their hands because they are

| one, two, three.

The lines are no longer there. The lines that tell their stories are replaced with smokestacks and pipelines that poison our bodies and the land.

She remembers the same form of violence inflicted on her body as the memory flickers through her eyes and is projected onto the back of her brain like the scene of a grainy old film where she was forced to buy a ticket. It is the memory of that not-so-innocent death that she was not supposed to witness

| witness this.

"It was an accident," they say.

She was just a "stupid fucking 'Indian' that had one too many drinks," they say.

"She tumbled down the stairs, step after step after step," they say.

| brain dead.

A single cord keeping her alive and her daughter is forced to decide. The memories she had are no longer alive and playing in her head, and her own personal truth is no longer able to survive.

But we know

| we know.

The truth outshines a lie but the liars refuse to figure out why. We are left without the answers to our questions and now no one talks. The silence is slowly killing us as we try to speak out loud, no words escape our mouths just big gasps for air as we try to remember her. She is the strong woman who lives on through her children and her grandchildren that she would never get to know.

She is there, within that little girl as she looks around and sees Creation gently scoop up her heart and tuck the tenderness safely within her chest, giving her a little nudge to go on. Her journey is not easy as she trudges through the heaviest mud on Earth that collects on the soles of her rough feet.

The veins of the earth below grab her tired worn-out body and try to pull her back in. She attempts to forget the ugliness she felt and for a moment thinks about sinking her body back into the earth. The memories are pulsing through her blood, making them more ingrained in her body with each breath she takes like the handprints she once left in the cement.

It is cold down below, but she feels the warmth of the sun spread across her face and she carries on. She can feel the strength of her ancestors rushing through her blood, reminding her that she is a survivor of all that has been done. She is here because they survived it all, and her heart screams as it is feeding from the strength above and below.

She now understands what needs to be done.

She grabs her heart with her tiny soft hands and squeezes too tight. She cannot bear the pain, but she knows she is alive because she can feel. The warmth of her hands spreads through her fingertips and she begins to create. She is unsure of what it is, but she puts trust in her bundle to be safe

| ready to let go.

She looks back, and the constellations of stars fill up the Longhouse behind her with her bundle safe in the middle. Her ancestors are there to remind her that they know exactly who she is

| they see her.

Creation is unearthed from the center of her heart as blood drips from her hands she begins to understand. She can feel the Constellations of Scars slowly turn into each and every single star, helping her body make its way back to her heart and her mind. She is no longer numb and starts to feel a pulse

| heartbeat.

It is the sound of all the women who give life to this earth. We must protect one another and push love through our hearts and scream

| "NO MORE!"

No more stolen sisters, no more stolen land, no more hate. We hold each other's hands as we rise. Rise for our children so they know their own strength as we breathe in and out like the tides of the waters, connecting to our grandmother. Exhale as this medicine washes away all the pain so all that remains is the resistance in our veins that screams out to those who will listen.

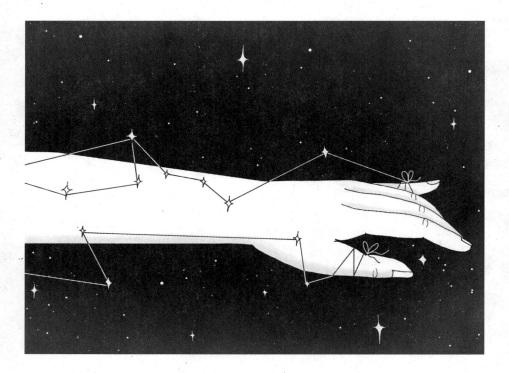

TOP 10 CRAZIES IN FICTION

by s.e. smith

It's my belief that the most authentic depictions of mental illness in fiction come from writers who have experienced mental health conditions themselves, which was my first criterion for inclusion on this list.

I also thought, though, about the notion that "any representation is a good representation." That's not a belief I share. Tired mental health stereotypes should be sent out to pasture to make room for lively, authentic, diverse writing about living with mental illness. That meant eliminating a lot of literal manic pixie dream girls, being quite choosy about trauma-induced mental health conditions, and thinking carefully about the messages sent by these books and these characters.

The experience of mental health is itself diverse. I didn't just rely on my personal opinion about great mentally ill characters; I sought insight and advice from mentally ill people across the young adult literature community. You may find that some of these books speak to you more than others. Some may conflict with your experience, or even feel hurtful—disagreeing with the inclusion of a given book doesn't make you wrong or bad. It makes you an informed, thoughtful reader with ideas other people probably need to hear.

Please note that many of these books include graphic descriptions of depression, anxiety, psychotic breaks, suicide, and other mental health topics.

- **AARON SOTO,** *More Happy Than Not* (Adam Silvera)

     This is a complicated book that explores depression—something Silvera knows well—but also sexuality and our relationship to society. If you could erase bad memories and be happy again, would you? Could you? There's a lot going on between the lines in this one.

- **BITTERBLUE,** *Bitterblue* (Kristin Cashore)

     Bitterblue marks an exception to my usual dislike of narratives featuring trauma-induced mental health conditions, because this is an emotionally complex presentation of post-traumatic stress disorder written by an author who's discussed her experience with anxiety. How does a kingdom recover after decades of abuse and gaslighting by an evil king? What kinds of emotional legacies has King Leck left behind, and how will Bitterblue put herself, and her kingdom, back together?

- **CRAIG GILNER,** *It's Kind of a Funny Story* (Ned Vizzini)

     Vizzini went straight to the source for this one: he based it on his own experiences in inpatient therapy. *It's Kind of a Funny Story* is, yes, funny, but also poignant and sad and relatable. If you've ever felt overwhelmed by the world around you, Craig will remind you that you're not alone.

- **ELIZABETH DAVIS** and **EMILY DELGADO,** *When Reason Breaks* (Cindy L. Rodriguez)

     Tired of hearing that there has to be some epic traumatic terrible reason for depression and suicide? So was Rodriguez when she wrote her debut novel, drawing upon her own experiences of depression in the Latinx community. Sometimes your brain just hates you, and *When Reason Breaks* is refreshingly frank about that.

- **KIRI BYRD,** *Wild Awake* (Hilary T. Smith)

     Smith's *Wild Awake* hit me right in the uncomfortable place, as it's such an intense, vivid description of what it is like to go crazy. One moment you are living a normal, reasonable life, and then something happens to throw you off-kilter and you are thrown into a riotous, out-of-control nightmare that wrenches you from everything you ever knew. The onset of mental illness isn't always so dramatic, but *Wild Awake* mirrors an authentic experience—especially given that many people start to develop symptoms of mental illness at Kiri's age. Smith, who once described herself as "mentally interesting" in an interview with me, understands firsthand what it is like to have your brain spin off into the stratosphere.

- **NORAH,** *Under Rose-Tainted Skies* (Louise Gornall)

  OCD and agoraphobia are often the subject of jokes, but Gornall knows personally that they're deadly serious. They're woven throughout this love story, which explores living with and trying to learn to manage mental illness, and affirms the fact that being crazy doesn't mean you're any less worthy of love. While there's a love story—spoiler alert—finding a boy doesn't magically fix Norah, and their journey isn't all smooth sailing.

- **SOLOMON REED,** *Highly Illogical Behavior* (John Corey Whaley)

  Whaley experiences anxiety and depression, and he brought that experience to bear in this lively, sometimes very funny story about living with acute agoraphobia. Solomon can't even leave his own house, a newfound friend is convinced she can fix him, and all hell is about to break loose in his life because no one around him really understands his illness and how to meet him halfway.

- **SOPHIE WINTERS,** *Far from You* (Tess Sharpe)

  In childhood, Sharpe experienced anxiety, depression, and several suicide attempts, and found her lifeline in young adult fiction. She returned the favor with *Far from You,* featuring Sophie, who is trying to figure out who killed her best friend after a life turned upside down by a car accident, a series of painful surgeries, and a dependence that became an addiction. I do wish to note, however, as did Sharpe herself when we discussed Sophie's depiction, that being dependent on pain management (or any medication) isn't wrong, and questions of addiction and abuse arise when a need (pain control) becomes a want (the psychoactive effects of opiates).

- **VICKY CRUZ,** *The Memory of Light* (Francisco X. Stork)

    I'm a huge fan of Stork, who experienced his first serious bout of depression in his teens. The "waking up in the hospital after a suicide attempt" story has been done a lot of times, but it's done well here. Vicky and the people around her come to life—and are at times pretty funny, dark, and sad—as she faces up to the "after" of her failed attempt.

WHAT WE'RE BORN WITH AND WHAT WE PICK UP ALONG THE WAY

by Heidi Heilig

It's strange to realize that, despite having an innate ability for it, I am actually terrible at being crazy.

How can one be so bad at something one is meant to be? Bipolar disorder is, after all, some combination of genes and their expression. *Maybe she's born with it. Maybe it's dopamine.* But despite this natural affinity for madness, I'm pretty sure I'm doing it all wrong.

Part of it must be that I am currently unmedicated, so, to put it mildly, there are some ups and downs. The world around me is often gilded in my eyes, but self-destruction lurks in my dark red heart. I'm often driven by hedonistic desire, but when I come down from that particular high, the repercussions—hangovers, credit card bills, high school accusations of being a slut, not to mention the shame of it all—are not half as much fun as the memory of the indulgence. And as many times as I've written a masterpiece on the back of a napkin while between subway stops, I've just as often sat staring at a blank page—or a blank wall—unable to summon a single word.

It hasn't always been this way. I was medicated for a while, and life was fine. Lovely, really. A lot of good things, very few bad. And things were certainly more stable. Why did I stop?

I'm still trying to understand that.

No, that's a lie—I know why I stopped; I was trying to get pregnant, and the medication I was taking was listed as Class D: adverse reactions have been found in humans. I didn't want adverse reactions (who does?), and I was pretty sure I could handle stepping down and then off my medication.

And I could. I can.

That's the thing. I'm one of the lucky ones. My disorder is comparatively mild. Being unmedicated is not a major risk for me. Which is probably why I never started back up again—or part of why anyway.

The rest of the reason I stopped medicating, like I said before, is that I'm just bad at being crazy. I would sometimes forget to take my pills. I hated seeing my doctors— not because they were bad doctors, but because I was A Bad Crazy. I mean, everyone knows the "right" way to be crazy is to develop a solid, trusting relationship with a professional, to keep taking your medications, and to avoid stress and triggers, right? That's what the newest books tell me anyway.

But back when I was a teen and just opening the Pandora's box of my bipolar disorder—an ugly family heirloom given to me when I hit puberty—things were very different. I grew up during the tail end of Gen X, and we had bands like Green Day in the nineties telling us not to be part of the Prozac Nation. Mental illness was portrayed as scary, and treatment for mental illness, even scarier. A decade ago, I remember seeing the musical *Next to Normal*, which featured a bipolar character who undergoes electroshock therapy in a frightening and very dramatic scene. The rest of the show, as I recall it, is about her destroying her family and flinging herself around the stage.

It was not easy to watch.

But I knew from movies that mania wasn't all that unattractive—the Manic Pixie is always a Dream Girl. From Shirley MacLaine in *The Apartment* (1960) to Penny Lane in *Almost Famous* (2000)—there seemed to be nothing sexier than a failed suicide attempt. It sounds ridiculous when I put it that way, but what is one glib sentence against a deluge of celebrated attempts at self-destruction?

When we aren't terrible mothers or self-destructive sex addicts, we can also be killers or villains: *The Shining* is a wonderful example of a murderous madman—even better, he's a writer. Just like me.

These days, especially in young adult fiction, there are more and more books that offer a nuanced and humanizing understanding of mental illness, and they are rightly praised. Teens are shown visiting with nonevil doctors and taking nonterrifying pills. Even better, they find hope! It's a strange new world for me to witness, and a beautiful one. Maybe someday I'll feel at home there.

IT'S A **STRANGE** NEW WORLD, AND A **BEAUTIFUL** ONE.

But I don't, not yet. The lessons I learned early have taken deep root, and it is hard to cultivate new ideas. I'm not sure why, though my guess is it has something to do with the malleable nature of intelligence in youth and the fact that our brains stop growing at age twenty. The younger you are, the easier it is to learn, for better or for worse.

These days, as an unmedicated—or occasionally, self-medicated—bipolar person, seeing the "right, responsible" way to handle my crazy is nearly as difficult as seeing the wrong way. It's a new standard that I can't quite live up to. And I'm one of the lucky ones who can afford doctors and medication. I can't imagine the pressure that those without my resources must feel, or the judgment they must face.

Because it is a judgment. Illness in general has a long history of being attributed to a flaw in the sick person's character or a punishment for their sins, and the media surrounding illness doesn't help. So often a villain is called crazy—or a crazy person is deemed a villain. Those of us who don't give our all for a cure—or more accurately, for control of our crazy—are seen as moral failures. Too lazy to do the right thing.

But should there be a "right" way to be crazy? Something in me resists that idea. Maybe because if there is a "right" way, there is a "wrong" way, and I'm sure I'm not the only one who can't do everything right. I want to believe less in judgment and more in contemplation—in an ongoing, evolving way to treat ourselves and each other that may or may not include professional treatment.

I suppose that illustrates the need for multiple narratives—so that people like me can finally internalize the myriad valid ways of existing. So that young people with their malleable, remarkable minds can fill them with many versions of their own bright futures, even if the shadows linger. So there can be a day when there is no "right" and no "wrong" to living with mental illness. There's just someone else's story.

SOME OF THE THINGS

MANIA ASSURES ME I COULD TOTALLY BE

by
Heidi
Heilig

—AND WOULDN'T IT BE GLORIOUS?

- PALEONTOLOGIST WHO DISCOVERS A MAJOR NEW SPECIES OF DINOSAUR

- CELEBRATED YET DOWN-TO-EARTH CHEF

- WILDLIFE PHOTOGRAPHER

- MINIMALIST

- A LITERAL MIND READER WITH POSSIBLY MAGICAL ABILITIES

- ANYTHING

- EVERYTHING

THE ALCHEMY OF HEALING

by Emily Mayberry

Everyone has experiences that shape who they become. Pivotal moments where every-thing slows and shifts; a dance of the push and pull of physics, emotions, and free will. For me, one of those moments shattered everything I thought I knew, all my security, all my trust in humanity. When it happened, and for a number of years after, I was quietly destroyed.

In time, I decided to take back my power, and my life. It took a lot of hard work.

It happened on an overcast Valentine's Day. I was walking to class on the Northern Illinois University campus, and my attention was drawn to a solemn figure: tall, skinny, in a trench coat, with a blank look on his face. I did not understand why this guy made my stomach turn and my heart race. I brushed the feeling aside and wondered why I was being so judgmental. A few hours later, the reason for my unease became all too real. And when I saw his face in the papers days later, my heart sank in recognition.

That day, I cut through Cole Hall, like I always did, to get to my next class on time. I noticed a woman holding an impossible stack of books and papers struggling to navigate the threshold, so I held the door open for her, then sauntered down the stairs. Suddenly, there were shotgun rounds ringing out on the other side of a classroom door. I turned to face the sound in disbelief, just in time to see the same woman I'd helped moments before throw the books and papers in the air. I saw her mouth move, but I could not process the sounds she was making. My mind was moving too fast. I watched the papers swirl and fall in slow motion. My instinct took over and I ran.

How many shooters are there? Where will I be safe? Am I going to die?

Questions in my head pounded as loudly as my heart, but I just kept running. I cut through an adjacent building so I could warn as many people as possible of the danger. I screamed, "There's a shooter—run!" Some people started running, but most looked confused. I ran for a long time because nowhere felt safe enough for me to stop; the construct of safety had been shattered. Finally, I came to a stop in a parking lot far away from campus. Helicopters were starting to fly in from every direction, sirens blared somewhere in the distance, and I tried to understand what had just happened. Was it even real?

I called my then boyfriend, the skater boy, and begged him to pick me up. It was not until I sat down on his couch that I started to sob. The news was on and I saw one of my friends on a stretcher. She did not look okay. Was anyone I knew dead?

The phone lines were jammed for hours. When I finally was able to call my mom, I was shaking. Hearing her voice on the other end was more comforting than anything in the universe. "I'm okay, Mom. I'm okay. It's all right. I'm okay." I repeated these words over and over until my mom coaxed what had happened out of me. I felt wrapped in the warmth of her love, and I was a little girl again, Momma melting away all my worries and pain in that crucial moment.

The next few days were a blur, and skater boy kept telling me I had no reason to be so upset; it wasn't like I had been in the classroom. I needed to get over it. I began to wonder if he was right.

Later that week, I was walking around in a store back home, and I could not help but notice that it felt like I was floating and not really in my body. Everything put me on edge. Loud noises made me jump with panic. At night, the sounds of the shotgun and of people screaming and wailing like animals haunted me. My imagination created images from what I had heard that day, and I ached for normalcy. It was a nightmare I could not wake up from.

When school opened two weeks later, I felt ready and eager to return. My first class was in an auditorium like the one where the shooting had happened. I took a deep breath, found a seat, and tried to act normal. But I couldn't. A spot on the back of my head started pounding and felt burning hot. My body was reacting to the paranoid thoughts gathering like a storm could. *That's where the bullet is going to go and that is where I am going to get shot*, my mind tried to convince me. I attempted to console myself, whispering sweetly that I was safe. Then there was a loud slam as someone burst through the door after class had already begun. That was my breaking point.

I could not stop the panic attack. I gathered my things and ran out of the room. Collapsing into a puddle in the hallway, I sobbed and shook until the feelings subsided. What was wrong with me? I kept telling myself it should not be so hard, that I did not need to react this way, that I thought I was stronger than this. There were grief counselors brought in for students who needed to talk, but I told myself they were for people who had been in the classroom. I had run. I did not get shot at. I did not go into the room to help anyone or try to stop the gunman. The guilt I felt was crippling.

Months went by and life seemed to level out and become familiar again. Through yoga asanas (poses) and meditation I was able to regain a sense of control. The familiar motions and connecting my heart with my breath eased the tension away. I spent a lot of time in nature talking with the Great Spirit, and I gained strength from the plants, breeze, and moving water. I could not bring myself to speak to humans about any of it. Instead, I moved slowly and let time and nature work at repairing my tattered spirit. I could laugh, feel at ease even, but there was always this subtle feeling of dread. I had brushed death and heard people dying. It changed the way I thought and felt, and impacted things inside me that I could not even understand yet.

During chorus practice a few months later, we were having trouble keeping time together on a new piece. My teacher had us stomp to stay together. The sound was loud and rhythmic and my heart started pounding. I was confused until hot tears began to well up in my eyes and I felt the need to run. Not just a need but a burning animalistic frenzy of a need to run. So I did. When I reached the hallway, I collapsed and cried, exhausted from my inability to move forward with my life. Every unexpected sound, strange-looking person, or anything that caught me off guard brought on a cocktail of adrenaline, anxiety, and paranoia. It was clear to me that I needed to do something to feel in control of myself more completely.

The opportunity presented itself when the university announced it was going to knock down Cole Hall. I was enraged. How could that be? The administration had not asked us, the students, if that is what we wanted or needed. What about how badly I needed—and perhaps other students did, too—to see that building as a part

I FELT **STRONG** FOR THE FIRST TIME IN SO LONG.

of the healing process? The university could not knock down a building and magically make the physical and psychic fallout go away. My frustration led me to join a group that was gathering signatures for a petition that would give us as students the right to hold a town hall–style meeting to vote on the future of the building. We stood outside for long hours in the cold of the MLK Commons. Right next to the student center, this open courtyard was teeming with people to engage with. Every student who stopped by and every faculty member I spoke with ignited my sense of purpose. I was finally able to help in some way, and it felt like by trying to save this building, I was able to find some sense of empowerment. I found my voice again. I felt strong for the first time in so long.

A Chinese news station was covering the petition and wanted to interview someone. Everyone else was reluctant, so I found myself stepping up to the plate. During that interview, I was asked the questions that had become so typical of interviews following tragedies like this, including how I now felt about gun control laws. I did not, however, give the typical answers. I offered hope, peace, and a wish to help heal the hurt people who could commit such acts. I spoke the clamoring of my spirit out loud: I named my feelings and, more important, I named my determination to get my power back and my refusal to remain a victim.

Our petition got over three thousand signatures, and we presented our proposition to the vice president of the school. Cole Hall is still standing to this day. The students spoke their wishes and voted to remodel parts of the building instead of tearing it down. The university even added a beautiful memorial sculpture and granite plaques at the front of the building.

Life gained meaning again over time, and the more I meditated and did inner work, the better I got. It was a slow process of literally rewiring my brain, but it was working. I was determined to not let this single experience take over my life. Yet, years passed and I was still set off easily, overreacting emotionally to situations and people in ways that did not make logical sense. My body was trying to get my attention and make me face what I needed to. Despite what I stubbornly thought, there was a part of me that knew I needed more help and could not do this alone anymore. I was sick of isolating myself. A part of me felt ashamed that I was still so deeply affected, and it seemed easier to keep my feelings inside. A bigger part of me realized, however, that enough was enough—I refused to half live my life.

A family friend was a counselor who practiced a type of therapy called eye movement desensitization and reprocessing (EMDR), and they had offered help if I ever wanted to try it. I am a firm believer in alternative healing methods, and even though this friend was a traditional counselor, this process was not at all typical. EMDR helps the mind process traumatic events and is often used with veterans to help with post-traumatic stress disorder (PTSD). The method helps take out the trauma from where it has been pushed down out of self-preservation and allows that trauma to be revisited and properly processed. Even though a number of years had passed since the incident, I still felt lingering effects of PTSD. I wanted to be free, so I dove in and gave EMDR a try. It was a beautiful experience. I was able to reframe my perception and beliefs about the shooting. I realized I had no reason to feel guilty. I also finally felt like I had stopped running, a sensation that had haunted me and kept me on edge.

I found my power again. Since I had been able to shift my perception of the shooting, it made me shift how I felt about the shooter himself. I forgave him and even found compassion for his pain after I looked into his story. As I learned how much he'd grappled with his own mental health, I was able to gain some understanding. He wasn't able to get the kind of help he needed or deserved. What he did wasn't a sign of our society breaking down. It was a cry for help and demonstrated a need for a reform to our approach to mental health. I learned all this by better understanding my own mental health, and this knowledge inspired and encouraged me to spread my message.

Sharing my experience became a large part of my healing process. I held workshops where people could come and use art or movement as a catalyst for change. I taught how I had used art to dig into, express, and thus better understand my emotions. Each month, I held poetry readings at the hookah lounge where I worked.

I was outspoken about refocusing discussion around school shootings from needing stricter gun laws to, instead, helping heal the broken people who were behind the guns. There are so many people who are pushed down and to the side, and then when they finally crack, we label them and cast them aside. How much pain and devastation could we avoid by fixing the root of the problem instead of cowering away in fear?

Through the mysterious ways of the web of life, I was given a bigger outlet for my message. After speaking my mind that day I gathered signatures for the petition, I was contacted time and time again for interviews. Through this willingness to share my story, I have been able to give voice to the traumas I experienced and to the wellness path that worked for me. These have been opportunities to further my healing and, hopefully, to help others on their journey.

Fast forward to nine years after the shooting occurred. I was asked to write this very piece, but I was stuck. And then I knew what I had to do. I needed to go back to where it all began to complete my healing process.

On a trip to the area near my old school, it dawned on me that it was a school day. I walked to Cole Hall and entered the front door. The first floor had been remodeled, so it looked different, but the setting was close enough for my purposes. My mind and spirit were ready but my body resisted. The panic rose with every step I took toward the door to the classroom where the shooting had occurred. My body shook violently, and my heart beat out of my chest. I lovingly coaxed my body forward, whispering that I was okay now. I collapsed—for what would be the last time—from the overwhelming emotions. I slowed and steadied my breath and gave myself the space to express what I needed to.

I walked over to what was now the door to a women's bathroom and stood right where everything had changed. Images, sounds, and emotions chaotically swirled in my head, but I stood firmly grounded, knowing it would pass. I sat down next to the door with my back pressed against the wall and let the process happen. I cycled through laughter, crying, fear, elation, and I felt like I was losing my mind. Yet I kept breathing, kept telling myself I was safe, and slowly, everything settled until all that was present was my calm breath. This was now just a hallway with students on their way to class, like it had been on that day—as well as the days that came before and after it.

I said a prayer for the lingering energy left from the trauma to clear. I prayed for everyone who was affected by the shooting. I prayed for peace and for the healing of all the wounded lost souls. I prayed for so many things.

My final step was to light some palo santo, which is used to energetically cleanse and bless spaces. I offered more prayer and felt all the remaining heaviness lift. The space was clear. I felt the land sigh with relief and I sighed with it.

Instead of leaving the space neutral, I wanted to leave a positive imprint, an energetic message. With deep intention, I picked up my sacred circle, my Hula-Hoop. Indigenous tribes dance with hoops to honor the circular and cyclical nature of life and the interconnectedness of everything, and I honor and embody all that when I dance with it. I called to my ancestors and felt them at my back. I danced in that hallway a dance of life, of celebration, of empowerment.

That day will always be a part of my story, but I have transmuted a story of fear and pain into a story of joy, strength, and love. I believe in every fiber of my being that everyone has the ability to do so if they believe in their own incredible power.

CHAPTER THREE

THE MIND–BODY CONNECTION

ON THE SURFACE, eating disorders and addictive behaviors seem completely different. Yet these two types of mental illness have a crucial thing in common: they impact the physical body as well as the mind.

Though no mental health experiences are universal, eating disorders and addictive behaviors are often also illnesses about control. Those who struggle with addiction and/or eating disorders seek a sense of control over uncontrollable situations through various unhealthy means. They may binge and purge. They may choose not to eat at all. Others may turn to alcohol and use it as a crutch through extended periods of their lives. But once the cycle is recognized, there is immense opportunity to heal both mentally and physically.

You can't talk about the physical body without also considering the mind. And when the mind is hurting, chances are, the body is, too.

BLESS THIS MESS

by Amy Reed

Sometimes I'm okay. Sometimes I am very far from okay. Sometimes I write novels about the not-being-okay, and sometimes those novels win awards. Sometimes those novels are big flops. Sometimes I feel like my whole existence is a big flop. Sometimes I forget the difference between what actually happened and what I made up for the novels. Sometimes I wish I made it all up for the novels. Sometimes I wish I could just close the book and put it on a shelf and be a normal person for once.

The thing is, there are no "normal" people. Let's get that out of the way. Another thing is that we are all suffering. Some of us just have more creative ways to do this suffering business. Some of us won the jackpot in terms of interesting brains, interesting families, interesting luck, interesting chaos. Some of us need more creative tools to make sense of it all.

I used to think chaos was always interesting, by definition—my chaos, your chaos, chaos in general. Some part of me still believes I'm in my early twenties and wild and beautiful and indestructible (despite all the destruction). I keep trying to pretend I'm young by getting more tattoos and age-inappropriate haircuts, but the truth is I'm pretty boring. I have a ton of gray hairs and I'm a mom and I'm tired all the time and I'm in my pajamas most nights by 7:00 p.m., and I spend a lot of my free time trying to be a better person. I'm also eight years sober.

But you know what's even more boring than my current day-to-day life? Death. Or even before death, there's the boring and repetitive chaos of addiction, repeating the same boring mistakes over and over again, telling the same boring lies. Relationships failing in the same boring ways, no matter how many times I changed schools or changed cities or changed drugs or took a break or did a cleanse or saw a therapist or fired a therapist or got a new boyfriend or got a new girlfriend. One after another, again and again, everything failed, while I got puffier and my body started doing scary things like having elevated liver enzymes, whatever the hell those are. I'm telling you, chaos is boring. And dangerous.

I have been to rehab twice, once when I was sixteen and once when I was twenty-nine. I may have ODed a couple times, but it's kind of hard to define ODing when you don't actually die.

No matter what's in my system, I have always been very high functioning, meaning I could make everything look good on the outside. Except for those possible ODs of course. Or maybe when I dropped out of college because I was so strung out. Or maybe all those many years I'd get drunk or high in secret, in the morning, at lunch, before class, before work, and thought no one could tell. Or how I'd hide bottles in the bottom of the recycling bin so my husband wouldn't know how much I drank. Or how I was so embarrassed on recycling day because the strangers who came by to collect bottles to return for five cents each would know my secret. They must have loved me.

Could anyone tell? Was I fooling anyone?

I am a well-educated, middle-class, pretty girl who usually passes as white, so I was fooling a lot of people. I got away with things people who are not middle-class white girls often do not get away with. I was too self-absorbed to realize any of this then, but I know now that my privilege protected me from consequences. This shames me now. But it also may have saved my life.

I fooled myself for a long time, despite the obvious signs. But that's the thing about being (mostly) high functioning—we're experts at fooling ourselves. I used my super organizational skills, perfectionism, and exceptional willpower to be the best alcoholic and drug addict I could be. I was a double agent. I would have been great in the FBI if I hadn't been so loaded. On the outside, I looked (mostly) fine. I went to work. I sounded smart. I even jogged and went to yoga sometimes. So what if I passed out every night? So what if I often could not remember what I did for the couple hours before I passed out?

Even when I went to rehab, I was high functioning. Both times, it surprised everyone. They did not know the extent of my talent for smiling when I was a tornado inside. At sixteen, despite my slightly problematic attendance record and that one time I passed out in math class during a group test, I was a straight-A student in honors classes. I'd get caught occasionally with drugs or breaking curfew, but I was a good liar and my parents desperately wanted to believe that it was "just this time," that I was "only experimenting," that I'd "never do it again."

I had a great group of friends in high school, many of whom were in my wedding and with whom I am still close today. They were the kids who experimented with me when they were young and grew out of it as adults. I was the one who did not grow out of it. They got high with friends and drank at parties. I was the one who was not doing it to party. I was not doing it to have fun. I got high, alone and without telling them, because it was the only way I knew how to function. It was the only way I knew how to feel safe in my body and deal with the thoughts and feelings plaguing my mind. By "deal," I mean "running away from."

It felt like someone snuck inside my brain, poked around, tangled up the wiring, made a mess, and suddenly it was my responsibility to clean it up. Maybe it was all those drugs I did. Maybe it was all that less-than-ideal parenting and trauma. Maybe it was the history of mental illness on my dad's side. Maybe it was thetans or demonic possession or karmic punishment for past-life transgressions.

My mind is still a mess today.

Drug addiction. Alcoholism. Major depressive disorder. Anxiety disorder. Post-traumatic stress disorder (PTSD). Panic attacks. You name it. My new therapist thinks I may have bipolar II. Add to that the hormonal birth control I started at age fourteen, and the new reports that it may lead to depression, and the fact that my teenage sui-cidal ideation always peaked for a day or two every month like clockwork. Basically, I have been a mess of brain chemicals, hormone chemicals, and drug chemicals for most of my life. I have been on Prozac, Paxil, Zoloft, Effexor, and Wellbutrin. I think there's another one I'm forgetting.

The first time I went to rehab, I was sixteen. I had spent the evening riding around my neighborhood in the back of my friend's truck getting high and trying not to get thrown around as he turned corners. By the time I got to rehab later that night, I was banged up and bruised from the truck ride, more tired and stupid than anything.

I had my guitar and a suitcase half filled with books, and I was ready for a nap. I thought I was going on vacation.

That's what I wanted: a vacation. A vacation from myself. That was essentially what I was looking for every time I got drunk or high, but those escapes had stopped working. Now I wanted a vacation from that failed vacation, and I wanted to play guitar and read novels during my getaway.

I remember doing my intake interview in a sleepy haze. Yes, I hid drugs. Yes, I used alone. Yes, I lied about how much I used. Yes, drugs had caused problems in my relationships and in school. Yes, I had used drugs to counteract the effect of other drugs. Yes, my life had become unmanageable.

They refused my guitar entry. The books I could keep, though I would not get many chances to read them. The thing about rehab is you are busy all the time. You sit in circles a lot. You talk and listen to other people talk. You ride in white vans to meetings in church basements full of old men who look at you suspiciously. You make therapeutic art projects. You watch movies about people getting sober. You do not get a lot of time to lie around and be the person you're used to being. Rehab is busy, but it is boring. Almost as boring as being a drug addict. It is not a vacation and certainly not a vacation from yourself.

I cannot smell Irish Spring soap now without getting a full-body memory of showering at rehab. I still have the Polaroid picture they took at Christmas: I'm sitting on Santa's lap (yes, Santa came to rehab), wearing my *Big Lebowski* sweater backward, my shoulder-length hair in the sad knots of attempted Asian/white girl dreadlocks. That evening, we got Christmas stockings full of sugar-free candy, then watched two episodes of a short-lived sitcom called *The John Larroquette Show*, starring John Larroquette as a recovering alcoholic. I still remember the theme song.

I gave the counselors what they wanted. I played my role and answered in character. I was the model rehab patient, just as I had been the model student. I wanted straight A's in recovery. I wanted to be the drug addict they could fix. I wanted to be fixable. I wanted them to shake me like a snow globe. I wanted to close my eyes and feel the tiny breeze of their wands doing magic around me, then I would emerge, my broken pieces fixed, and we'd never have to speak of it again.

But of course it is more complicated than that. There is that whole thing about addiction being a disease that never quite goes away. There is that whole thing about my entire existence being a series of cravings and attachments and aversions and seeking pleasure and trying to avoid pain. There is my depression to consider. My anxiety. My nervous attachment style. My inability to communicate. My trauma. The countless shadows that trail me wherever I go, picking up debris, making a mess.

The thing about being a mess is you think you have two options: you have to clean yourself up or you keep hoping someone else will do it for you. (Spoiler alert: someone else can never do it for you, as much as you—or they—might want them to.)

The thing about getting clean is that once you get out of rehab, no one's getting paid to take care of you anymore. That is when the real work starts. At sixteen, I was not ready to do the real work, so my sobriety did not last long. But a seed was planted. Somewhere inside, behind the shadows, I knew there was a solution if I wanted it. I knew there was a path and there were tools to end my suffering if I became willing to tell the truth and do the real work. But as they say in the rooms of recovery communities, I had more research to do.

That leads me, I suppose, to this writing business. Living in my addiction was research for my recovery, which is in some ways similar to how a writer's life is research for their writing. I did a lot of one kind of living, and my first several novels reflect that. I've written a lot about addiction, about mental illness and trauma, about lost souls desperate for connection, about being your own worst enemy. I've relied a lot on my experiences as a teen and young adult for the subjects of my novels. My first two novels in particular, *Beautiful* and *Clean*, are very autobiographical.

But I almost did not become a writer. Ironically, it was writing essays much like this one—messy nonfiction about my own messy life—that almost ended my dream of becoming a writer.

I took a creative nonfiction workshop in college, not too long before I dropped out. The teacher did not like my writing. He liked poems and essays, with big words, about mountains. He did not like confessional writing. I wrote about the mess in my head. I confessed all over the place. I desperately wanted someone to listen.

Paper had always listened. When I was young and full of shame and loneliness, I could write down my pain and the paper took it. The paper listened when I was thirteen and so terrified I could barely speak, when I was already getting high by myself to avoid the mess in my head, the mess in my heart, the pain of having no one I felt safe telling, the pain of having no control over what people did with my body. But *I* had control over the substances I put in my body; I thought that gave me control over my feelings. I learned quickly that control was false. But no matter what happened, I always had control over what I put on the paper.

This is why I almost quit writing forever: an anonymous student in my creative nonfiction class wrote a letter and put it in my campus mailbox. The letter told me my essays were a cry for help and had no place in a writing workshop. When I told my teacher about the letter and how much it hurt me, he didn't care. And maybe the student was right. Maybe I did need help, maybe I was unmedicated and had just started the exciting new experience of chronic panic attacks, maybe I got high every day and was on the hunt for something stronger, maybe I was sleeping with a guy I couldn't stand but felt desperate to keep, maybe I was so desperate for someone to listen that I vomited my secrets all over those unsuspecting creative writing students and expected them to workshop *me*, to validate my suffering by saying it was art.

My suffering was not art. It was just suffering. It was untreated mental illness and drug addiction and PTSD and a little girl trapped in the body of a young woman who was screaming for strangers to see her because the people who mattered to her never could.

I quit writing for many years after that. But as I began a slow climb to wellness in my late twenties (a climb that will never be over, by the way), writing came back to me. Or I came back to writing. Or I came back to myself. Or meds and therapy and another stint at rehab finally worked, and I finally claimed a confidence in my voice that no weird anonymous letter from a creative writing student telling me my writing was the rantings of a crazy person could crush.

Maybe all the confessing I've done behind the safety of fiction really has helped all those readers who have emailed me saying my books helped them feel less alone, helped them ask for help, helped them clean up their messes, helped them save their own lives.

Maybe that is the point of all writing—to communicate, to connect, to forge compassion and understanding between writer and reader. Not to impress some elitist writing professor. And sometimes that communication comes out as a confession. And maybe that's okay. Because maybe confessing is better than keeping it all in. Maybe telling secrets is better than letting those secrets fester and poison us and make us sick. Even when they're cries for help. Maybe *especially* when they're cries for help.

Maybe it's true that I could have been more selective about who I told my secrets to. Maybe a writing workshop full of immature strangers and a macho teacher who hated "women's writing" was not the right venue for my confessions. That's the thing about being someone who only ever knew how to keep secrets, who never learned how to communicate—we may not always know how to start; we may not be the best judges of when and where it is safe to be vulnerable. But you know what? There is a fine line between foolish and brave, and sometimes our actions can be both. I was trying to be brave. I was trying to let people in. I was trying.

I am who I am today because of my messes. Because I've survived them. Because I've written about them. Because I've learned from them, because I keep searching for new tools to clean them up, because I keep trying to heal. And maybe healing makes me boring. Maybe running and meditation and motherhood and sobriety and eating vegetables and working hard at this writing thing makes me boring. But I'll take it. If I need unboring, I'll create it on paper. I'll navigate messes with my characters. I will help them find the tools for cleaning up their messes. I will open up my heart and put it in my books for you, and maybe when you open up my books, you will read something that feels true. You'll know you're not alone, and you'll know it's okay to not feel okay all the time—and maybe you'll find something in these pages that helps you clean up your messes, too.

LOOSENED ASSOCIATIONS

by Esmé Weijun Wang

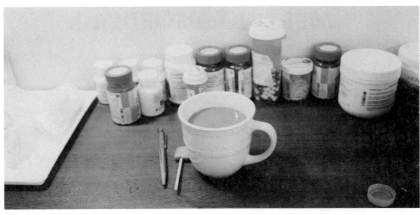

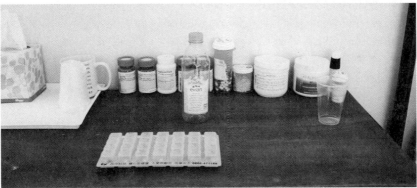

During psychotic episodes, because the concepts of both myself and
the world around me are so fragmented and untethered from reality, I
often cope by shooting with an SX-70 Polaroid and a Contax T2 camera.
It is important to me that taking pictures during a psychotic episode
includes the use of physical film, which is tangible in a way that
digital photographs are not.

MEETING DISORDER

by Jessica Tremaine

This is kind of ridiculous, but it all started exactly the way I tell parents these things never happen.

I got the idea from a book.

It wasn't even like it was a book that I loved, or even liked very much. The main character was mildly annoying and a ballet dancer; I was neither. If anything, as the kind of kid who complained to the teacher when losing a point for neatness brought me down to 99 from a possible 100, I was probably *really* annoying.

I didn't enjoy the reading experience. And yet . . . I read that book over and over again.

The book-girl wanted to be perfect—she was under pressure; I thought I was, too. I was tasked with "doing my best" at school, and it was understood that "my best" would result in top grades. I was good at schoolwork, but the message was that there was always room to be better. I embraced that. I was competitive, and I wanted to win at things, especially things that I was already on my way to winning.

The book-girl would push the food around on her plate, and she'd divide sticks of gum into tiny doll-sized parcels; the result seemed so neat and orderly. So perfect-like. I wanted to be orderly and together. I wanted the inner me to be worthy of permanent display, like a diorama. The self I wanted to shake off was a little messy and prone to finishing projects at the last minute, rushing onto the school bus with the glue dripping from a tower of toothpicks, slightly askew. There was a discipline that called to me from the book-girl's life. Some part of me imagined that learning to have that sort of control would transform me into the type of girl who did not find old permission slips and bread crusts crumpled up in the bottom of her backpack. Who was not obsessively anxious about loss, even in the middle of abundance.

I wasn't even aware of being chubby until I made a triumphant fifth-grade return to a school that I'd left in third grade, a year when my true self had apparently been suffocated by the weight of my own flesh. On my first day back, the principal and my second-grade teacher crowed over how I'd "lost the baby fat." They had me pose and twirl for them repeatedly, in the middle of the principal's office.

I remembered this moment recently; it wasn't a happy memory.

But at the time I returned to that school, I was overjoyed. For one thing, I got to check out the principal's office, a place that I had not previously frequented (that was the goal), and for another . . . the principal and teachers were *noticing* me. Not my excellent grades, not my good manners, but my *self*, my body.

Me.

In eighth grade, my father was at home less, and my mother cried frequently. There seemed to be so much wrong, and nothing I could do to make things better. Age thirteen brought with it a sense of being unfamiliar with my own body, of a lack of control over myself, of no longer being sure who that "self" really was. I wanted to be simultaneously bound for the honor society and prom queen, but the paths seemed divergent and rough terrain for an awkward amateur like me. During a time when I desperately wanted to unveil a "new" identity, I remained brace-faced, bespectacled, someone who didn't visit the principal's office, and—to my mind—boring.

My friends and I spent afternoons at the mall, sharing packs of hot salty fries and chatting about "diets," and about how terrible we looked while also assuring each other that we were "perfect." Maybe they understood it as light chatter. Maybe they believed the slogans and PSAs that told us that everyone was beautiful in their own way. Or maybe, I thought, they just didn't want it enough. *I* did. I knew I could do better, be better, be *the best*, and win.

My attempts at plate organization and extreme portion control went unnoticed by my family, and my weight stayed the same. Around that time, I graduated to sticking my index finger down my throat. I'd gorge on bags of Doritos, boxes of doughnuts (the cinnamon-sugar ones were the best), and cherry Coke, eating quickly and secretly—grabbing two hot dogs and wolfing them down in the bathroom before I ate one in public at a relatively normal pace. Sometimes it took only a casual conversation about diets and supermodels to help me find my way to others who fought food like I did. One day, a friend told me that a quick-and-dirty weekend of weight loss was a breeze with Ex-Lax, and lots of it. "It's just like eating Hershey's," she said, her blond curls bouncing. She was skinny. I smiled and nodded, but it was much more satisfying, and purposeful, it seemed to me, to throw up right away, before the food "took." I imagined that whatever I ate would immediately turn into nasty white globules of pus-looking fat, visible remnants of failure. Getting rid of it right away meant that the bingeing, the hunger, my sloppy greed had never happened. Puking it up instantly was like hard work and magic. It was the best of both worlds.

My peers were all "WOW—YOU LOOK AMAZING!" anytime I happened to drop a couple of pounds, and silent when those pounds (inevitably) came back. When we took class pictures, I wasn't sure how to feel when the photographer's assistant said, "Whoa, I thought you'd be much fatter, from your head shot!"

Uh, thanks?

I took my eating pathology to college, along with my giant stuffed animals and dreams of carefree living like the pictures in college brochures. It didn't take long for me to realize that it was very difficult to be "in control" on a campus of twenty thousand superstars. I was not the smartest kid in the room anymore, and minor roles in high school plays did not make me the most talented. With two ill family members at home, and a father who had moved out, not only had I *not* shaken off my messy self but it began to feel like I would never be able to. That it was time to give up on perfection, and just . . . disappear. Rather than get help in class when I didn't understand, I stopped showing up. When I was assaulted, I absorbed the pain until it became shame. I convinced myself that people who had everything in order and under control didn't let their lives get like this. I was losing. I had already lost. I tried not to let it show. I listened to my friends' freshman struggles, and I worked hard to develop a reputation as a sage dispenser of advice and kindness to disguise my own ineptitude. I painted over the anxiety, uncertainty, and sheer terror that are a part of growing up with a hard, clear veneer of Cool Girl.

But when my first-semester grades came in, it was clear that there were cracks. It was time for me to take control. I got off the meal plan, for which my school was famous, and through which it was customary to binge on ice-cream sundaes and breaded chicken after a pizza appetizer, and I began to shop and cook for myself. In much the same way that I would manipulate and push around the food on my plate in my amateur days of Ordering

My Way Through a Food Disorder, I came upon a simple but brilliant strategy for cooking delicious and elaborate meals for my friends and "myself." I kept busy, looked accomplished, made people happy, and reveled in praise. Friends asked for tips on how to make pasta sauce without using Ragú or other ready-made items. I really enjoyed cooking: it was a stress reliever, and . . . I. Was. Really. Stressed. Out. So I cooked, but what I didn't do was eat. My cooking routine was lauded, and there was little that I liked better than praise. Refusing to eat, I felt simultaneously dainty and strong. Skinny me got *lots* of compliments.

Once you get to a certain place of not eating, it feels almost like a spiritual experience. It *is* a spiritual experience for many who fast for religious reasons. Your stomach shrinks, so you stop feeling as hungry. You feel proud of yourself for not succumbing, for not being weak, for the willpower, the control. Though so many things in my life were falling apart, I had it together. I was proud of myself. My grades went up. I had a boyfriend. I walked everywhere; I was good at *seeming* healthy. I could make an impressive lasagna—at least, that's what I was told. It did look good when I pushed it around on my paper plate.

The truth was, it finally felt like I was doing something right. Almost everyone around me was like that principal and that second-grade teacher. I was repeatedly rewarded with compliments for making myself less. For disappearing a little more every day.

There were times I ate food that other people cooked, though. My car made it easy for me to take solitary late-night trips to an all-you-can-eat buffet, where I binged on potato wedges and cheap slabs of "steak." And there was the most glorious of grocery stores, with the most superb selection of prepared foods, where I'd buy tubs of hot macaroni and cheese that I finished before I even got back to the car.

On a trip home, my best friend said, "You look amazing!" I was long and lean, "like a rope," he pointed out. I pretended that those words didn't feel like a noose.

But I slipped up.

I made a trip to a local diner with a group of friends, the way normal people did. After a tasty plate of clam strips—the kind of food that was small enough to not feel like food—I ordered a five-scoop ice-cream sundae, something I usually ate in minutes at 2:00 a.m., standing up in the dark. This time, I enjoyed it out in the open while we laughed and talked. I don't know if I finally felt like the girl I wanted to be or if a part of me wanted to "slip up." To drop the facade and be seen as I truly was. Maybe there was a tiny part of me, that messy, real me, that was not going to give up, not going to let my self completely disappear. When it was time to go, I stood up and my skirt . . . dropped down.

I grabbed it before it got to my ankles, but it fell fast and far enough that I was glad I had on good underwear. We screamed with laughter the way you do so that everyone can stare and wonder if they'll ever have as much fun. And we left. I could feel my friend H. glance at me from time to time as we rode home in my car. I made sure not to catch her eye.

I had lost so much weight that my skirt had literally dropped off me. Overloaded with classes, boyfriend woes, family worries, and more, I hadn't realized that I'd lost *that* much weight. While I was no longer puking up a storm, I didn't think about the fact that I cooked as part of an elaborate ruse to trick myself out of eating or that I ate whole cows and vats of congealed pasta and fake cheese in minutes, only to spend hours "paying for it" with endless hikes across the huge and hilly campus until I could feel empty again. I hadn't thought about what this meant about my body, about who I thought I was.

After that night at the diner, I knew that I couldn't fool anyone anymore, including myself. At school, I was a trained peer educator, and preparing for a work-study job coordinating programs and advising students. I had perfected my technique as a certified late-night "listener," nodding and murmuring gentle advice, offering home-made snacks and cups of tea. I knew how to handle this for others, and now it was time to work it out for myself.

I went and got help.

Getting help meant I did everything I never did before—I let myself be. I acknowledged the space that I took up, even though it seemed like so much more than it should be. I told the truth about how I was feeling, about my fears, my anxieties, my anger, my confusion. About the stress and the guilt, the strain in my ever-ready smile. About the things that I thought I should do and be, and how I would keep moving them just out of reach, so that doing my best would never be enough. I spoke the truth into visibility: No matter how good I thought I made it all look, one day my skirt was going to drop off, and what would be left would be me. Just me. There, for everyone to see. And what would I do then?

Now it was my job to figure out how to make me enough. How to do my best and be okay with not winning. How to satisfy my appetite for control, for perfection, without slowly destroying my body.

Years later, I'm still figuring it out. I'm still reminding myself that I need help, and that is okay. That I need to have people around me who will love and support me. Who let me know what I need to know because they *see me* and still love me. Who will help me look for myself when I get lost. That I'm not in control of everything, I never was, and I never will be. That somebody knows the me nobody knows, and they love me anyway.

More than anything, I really need that somebody to be me.

I'm not in charge—not even close—of all the things I thought I could control, and I'm okay. Most of the time, I can eat without counting, without silently berating myself for being weak, without believing with all my heart that I don't want to be worth my weight in anything because that would be too much.

I can eat almost everything in moderation and sometimes out of moderation. I can know that I have so much to be sad about, and joyful about, and afraid of, and angry because of, and I don't have to fix it all, or fix myself with food. I can let my life be what it is, and my *self* be who I am. I can muddle through.

Sort of.

Sometimes I look in the mirror and remember that girl. The one who looked "amazing."

And I wonder.

She's stronger than she looks. She might win. Even though I've learned and I know that I know better . . . she might win.

And then maybe I cut a cookie into four equal parts, and eat it slowly. Or I walk for miles, until the rising panic subsides.

I don't throw up.

I won't throw up.

Even when sometimes I really, really want to.

Still.

I'm working on it.

That girl in the book isn't me. I saw myself in parts of her story, but my own story is so much more. My story is beautiful. I can't skip to the ending, but I believe that my story *looks amazing*—all of it! And it's not finished yet.

I'll be okay.

I UNDERWENT COSMETIC SURGERY FOR *MY BODY* DYSMORPHIA . . . AND I WISH I HADN'T

by Reid Ewing

Body dysmorphic disorder is a mental illness in which a person obsesses over the way he or she looks. In my case, my looks were the only thing that mattered to me. I had just moved to LA to become an actor and had very few, if any, friends. I'd sit alone in my apartment and take pictures of myself from every angle, analyzing every feature.

After a few years of doing this, one day I decided I had to get cosmetic surgery. "No one is allowed to be this ugly," I thought. "It's unacceptable."

In 2008, when I was 19 years old, I made my first appointment to meet with a cosmetic surgeon. I genuinely believed if I had one procedure I would suddenly look like Brad Pitt.

I told the doctor why I felt my face needed cosmetic surgery and told him I was an actor. He agreed that for my career it would be necessary to get cosmetic surgery. He quickly determined that large cheek implants would address the issues I had with my face, and a few weeks later I was on the operating table. He spoke with me before I went under, but he wasn't the same empathetic person I met with during the consultation. He was curt and uninterested in my worries, making small talk with his staff as I lost consciousness.

I woke up screaming my head off from pain, with tears streaming down my face.

The doctor kept telling me to calm down, but I couldn't. I couldn't do anything but scream, while he and his staff tried seemingly to hold back their laughter.

Something I was not told ahead of time was that I would have to wear a full facial mask for two weeks. Afraid someone would find out I had work done, I took my dog and some supplies, left Los Angeles, and headed to Joshua Tree. I got lost on the way and stopped at a gas station in the middle of the night. It was closed, but I saw someone inside. Knowing I looked strange, I gently knocked on the store window, trying to look as unthreatening as possible. When the man saw me, he drew back in terror. He immediately grabbed the phone to call the police (at least that's what I assumed). I ran back to my car and drove off.

For the next two weeks, I stayed at a hotel doped up on hydrocodone. When the time came to take off the bandages, it was nothing like I had expected. My face was so impossibly swollen, there was no way I could make any excuse for it. So I planned to hide out in my apartment in LA for another week until the swelling was less dramatic.

On the way home, a cop pulled me over for a broken taillight. When she came to the window, we stared at one another in bewilderment. She asked what happened to my face, and I said I had been in a car accident. She went back to her car and got a Polaroid camera and took a picture of me. She let me off without saying much else, but I couldn't help imagining she would show the picture off back at the station, and that one day it would surface and ruin me.

After all the swelling finally went down, the results were horrendous. The lower half of my cheeks were as hollow as a corpse's, which, I know, is the opposite of what you'd expect, as they are called cheek implants. They would be more aptly called cheekbone implants.

I went back to the doctor several times in a frenzy, but he kept refusing to operate on me for another six months, saying I would eventually get used to the change. I couldn't let anyone see me like this, so I stayed in complete isolation. When I went out, people on the street would stare at me, and when I visited my parents they thought I had contracted some illness.

Unable to take this state of living, I began to seek out another doctor. The next one I found was even less qualified, but I didn't care; I just wanted out of my situation. I told him my story, and he suggested I get a chin implant. I asked if it would repair my sunken-in face, and he said I would be so happy with my looks it wouldn't matter to me. The same day he brought me into his back office and operated on me.

Like before, I went into hiding post-surgery. Only a few days passed when I noticed I could move the chin implant under my skin, easily moving it from one side of my face to another. I rushed back to the surgeon, and acknowledging he had made a mistake, he operated on me again. After the surgery, he waited with me while the anesthesia wore off so I could drive home. We had a heart-to-heart conversation, and he shared that it had been difficult to keep his practice open with the two lawsuits he was currently fighting.

ALL THE ISOLATION, SECRECY, DEPRESSION, AND SELF-HATE BECAME TOO MUCH TO BEAR.

At this point I was twenty years old. For the next couple of years, I would get several more procedures with two other doctors. Each procedure would cause a new problem that I would have to fix with another procedure. Anyone who has had a run-in with bad cosmetic surgery knows this is true. In terms of where I got the money to fund my procedures, it may not be as expensive as you would think. The new business model for cosmetic surgeons is to charge less and get more people in and out. I used the money I saved from acting and then borrowed from my parents and grandmother when I was most desperate.

Much of this was going on during the same time period I was shooting *Modern Family*. Most of the times I was on camera were when I'd had the numerous implants removed and was experimenting with less noticeable changes to my face, like injectable fillers and fat transfers. None of them last very long or are worth the money.

At the beginning of 2012, all the isolation, secrecy, depression, and self-hate became too much to bear. I vowed I would never get cosmetic surgery again even though I was still deeply insecure about my looks. It took me about six months before I was comfortable with people even looking at me.

Of the four doctors who worked on me, not one had mental health screenings in place for their patients, except for asking if I had a history of depression, which I said I did, and that was that. My history with eating disorders and the cases of obsessive-compulsive disorder in my family never came up. None of the doctors suggested I consult a psychologist for what was clearly a psychological issue rather than a cosmetic one or warn me about the potential for addiction.

People with body dysmorphic disorder often become addicted to cosmetic surgery. Gambling with your looks, paired with all the pain meds doctors load you up on, make it a highly addictive experience. It's a problem that is rarely taken seriously because of the public shaming of those who have had work done. The secrecy that surrounds cosmetic surgery keeps the unethical work practiced by many of these doctors from ever coming to light. I think people often choose cosmetic surgery in order to be accepted, but it usually leaves them feeling even more like an outsider. We don't hear enough stories about cosmetic surgery from this perspective.

Not long after I had decided to stop getting surgeries, I saw the first doctor I met with on a talk show and then in a magazine article, giving tips on getting cosmetic surgery. Well, this is written to counter his influence. Before seeking to change your face, you should question whether it is your mind that needs fixing.

Plastic surgery is not always a bad thing. It often helps people who actually need it for serious cases, but it's a horrible hobby, and it will eat away at you until you have lost all self-esteem and joy. I wish I could go back and undo all the surgeries. Now I can see that I was fine to begin with and didn't need the surgeries after all.

This piece was previously published in *Huffington Post*.

FLATTENED

by Susan Juby

I'm fourteen and at my friend's pool party. Her whole family is there. We've stolen booze from our parents' liquor cabinets and as usual I'm the drunkest. I love how uninhibited I feel, how socially skilled! Goodbye Corporal Dork, hello Colonel Charisma! My mind is always awash in stories, but they are more exciting when I'm drinking.

The story I come up with partway through the evening is that it would be fun to pretend that I can't swim. The plan is the product of a Drunk Mind, so it's not completely coherent. For instance, I have not worked out an explanation for why I have been swimming like an ungainly otter for most of the night. No matter. The main point is that I will be dramatically rescued from near drowning, and that will be enjoyable for everyone. When the time feels right, I walk along the edge of the pool and tip sideways into the water. No one notices. I float facedown and wait for someone to rescue me. The shouts, when they come, are intensely satisfying. Someone hauls me up and out of the water and makes sure I'm breathing. Exciting!

The whole saved-from-drowning thing goes over so well, I pretend-drown myself two or three more times. The third time, I hear someone say maybe they should just let me die already. Someone else notes out loud that the butt of my white bathing suit is see-through. I'm sure people were staring, openmouthed at my antics, but I didn't notice. I'm in the middle of a compelling Drunk Mind story and have no time to worry about what's happening around me. While I am being hauled out of the pool yet again, I hear my friend's handsome older brother ask his parents: "What is *wrong* with that girl?"

Excellent question. *What is wrong with me?*

I am nineteen and finally allowed to drink legally in Canada. Am quickly turning into a baby bar star. This particular night, I fall while leaving the dance floor of the local nightclub.

The handsome bouncer, new to our small town, helps me up. He's ridiculously fit, with biceps that strain his T-shirt sleeves. His blue contacts are slightly out of alignment with the dark eyes beneath. His Chinese accent is barely detectable but delicious. Unfortunately, he's so new to the scene that he doesn't know not to be direct.

"Why do you always drink so much?" he asks, setting me back on my feet.

I stare at him. I've turned into a blackout drinker but am in the midst of an unmerciful moment of consciousness. Thoughts flash through my addled brain like electrical shocks.

#1: *God, dude. I can't believe you just asked me that! Why don't you just punch me in the face while you're at it?*

#2: *I can't drink less. Trust me. I have tried.*

#3: *Look, I'm learning to drink like a normal person. Any day now I'll get it.*

I say nothing and go to the bar to get another drink.

I am twenty. I have moved away from my small town to one of the biggest cities in the country to attend college. The problem isn't my drinking, which is admittedly a little messy and excessive. The problem is my environment and people being all *judgmental and causing me artistic stiflement.* I can't thrive in a backwater where everyone is trying to hold me back and whatnot. I'm convinced the stimulation of an urban setting will set me free from my drinking and everything else.

Six months later, I have to quit my fashion design program because I have spent every cent of my student loan to buy alcohol and drugs.

To mark the last day of classes, and the end of my plan to become a costume designer for film and TV, I take an innocent classmate to a tacky male strip club near our school. There I get poisonously drunk on Long Island iced teas. The dingy club is located up two steep flights of stairs. On our way out, I fall down those stairs and end up lying in a heap in the street. I am badly bruised but I get up and keep going.

The next afternoon, a roommate knocks on my door and asks if I'm okay, which feels nearly as bad as when the hot bouncer asked me why I drink so much. I've spent all day hiding in my bed and smoking on the fire escape. I can't control my full-body shakes and I'm seeing things that aren't there.

Am I okay? I honestly don't know what I am anymore.

It's a week or so later, Christmastime, and I've gone back home. I haven't told anyone that I've dropped out of school. Instead, I attempt to play the role of ultraso-phisticated city person visiting the quaint village of her youth. I wear peculiar wide-legged plaid pants. My skin has turned the color of liver failure, and I hide it with a lot of foundation.

I plunge into an endless round of drugs and drinking. On New Year's Eve, I get in a fight in the worst bar in town, and me and my plaid pants are thrown out onto the snowy sidewalk by the bouncers while the band watches in amazement. I lie on the cold sidewalk for a while, momentarily shocked sober. The feeling of crusty snow against my cheek is almost enjoyable.

It's spring and I've been back in the city since January. I start drinking in the early afternoon even though I promised myself a few days before that I was going to quit. The last episode was bad, a lot like the episode before it and the episode before that. Somehow, each incident is fractionally worse. In fact, I've been trying with all my might to quit, but it's not working. I keep *not* quitting. I am unable to *remember* that I want to stay sober. I don't get a chance to think about whether I'm going to drink. I just do. It's terrifying, like my entire being has been hijacked.

A couple of hours later, I get separated from my friends when we change bars. I'm wobbling my way along a major street, alone. In the last couple of months, my abil-ity to stay mobile while seismically drunk has started to fail. I've always fallen a lot but was famous for leaping up and acting as though nothing had happened. No more. Sure enough, as I stagger down the street, my legs go out from under me and I hit the ground, hard, and roll over onto my back. I can't figure out how to get up, so I just lie there like an overturned turtle. A drunk one.

Crowds of people walk around me. Most avoid looking. Others gaze down, faces filled with pity and a hint of revulsion. I am the kind of drunk girl that people walk over.

It's July and I've finally asked for help. It's come from all sorts of quarters. I've been sober for three weeks. I'm twenty years old and this is the longest I've stayed sober since I was thirteen. I wake up in my bed to see sunlight streaming in through the battered blinds. I get up and open them and stand there, basking in the warmth of the new day. A strange buoyancy fills my chest. I realize it's hope.

It's June the following year. I'm twenty-one and I'm supposed to tell a whole roomful of people how I stayed sober for twelve whole months.

"I can't do this. I'm going to pass out," I tell the patient woman who has by this point spent countless hours listening to me bitch and moan and confess and cry and sometimes laugh.

"If you faint, we'll pick you up," she said. "It's not like you haven't fallen before."

It's been many years since that night, and I still fall sometimes, but at least now it's not because I've had too much to drink. And there's always someone there to help me up.

DEAR 14-YEAR-OLD MILCK

by MILCK

Dear 14-year-old MILCK,

You are enough. Just as you are.

You are not a bad person because you have anorexia and body dysmorphia.

You are not an unworthy person because you've become skilled at folding, editing, and positioning every little detail about yourself in the hopes of being accepted.

It is normal to feel both gratitude and shame for your ability to camouflage. Deep down inside, you feel relief for concealing "your inner monster," but at the same time, there's a part of you that knows you are *not* a monster. And a part of you doesn't want to settle for pleasing and appeasing. You are capable of so much more.

What you are doing, however, is endangering yourself by being too good at hiding your pain, starving yourself to feel like you have control. Your weight has dropped almost to ninety pounds, which is too skinny for your glorious five-foot-four-inch frame.

Notice the signs: The texture of your nails is becoming bumpy and thin because of malnutrition. And when you stand up from your desk at fourth period and get dizzying stars in your eyes, it's because your body is asking for more food.

I can tell you now that you are actually thinner than some of the girls in the magazines that haunt you, but your body dysmorphia warps your vision—you feel fat and gross, even when you're dangerously thin.

You'll see in time that the anorexia was a way to feel control while being overwhelmed by a restlessness that haunts you.

It's hard to know where the restlessness stems from. Sometimes it comes from hurt in the past. Remember your very first ballet performance at age eight? Recall the rush of adrenaline when you pushed past your stage fright, and you found that being onstage was exhilarating and magical? It felt like home, yes? After the performance, though, people called you the chubbiest ballerina onstage.

Mourn the pain your eight-year-old self felt, and embrace the pain you feel now. Howl and release. Then move on. Don't let the Muggle-like thoughts dim your magic, dear! Remember the feeling you had onstage, before you heard the intrusive remarks. You didn't give a rat's ass about your appearance. You were solely focused on the joyful stuff, like conquering your fears and exploring the stage. You'll get back to that mindset. It'll take a bit, but you'll get there.

You see, women of the previous generation, and from your culture especially, were extremely pressured to being thin, beautiful, and polite sidepieces for others. These standards have made many lionesses feel caged in, creating a poison of silent rage that courses through the veins, generation after generation. So when adults tell you that you are too chubby, too loud, too goofy, too emotional, or too idealistic, let those words melt off your skin. Hurtful words usually belong to those who haven't yet healed from the pain inflicted by their own demons.

The pressures of the previous generations still linger in your era. You'll also get drawn in by the physically flawless women posing in the beauty magazines. The cycle of unattainable perfection continues. The media is still too limited in the scope and portrayal of the ideal woman who is intimidatingly tall, thin, sexy, and wealthy, so don't be surprised if beauty magazines actually make you feel ugly.

Those unrealistic photos are trying to sell you something. They are designed to make the readers feel lesser than so that they will want to buy those products, to *aspire* to being like the well-dressed models they see in the magazines. Real people don't look like that. And you are real. You are beautiful, and have the potential to shine your genuine, loving light into the world.

The best way for you to begin to heal and to rise above the oppressive pressures surrounding you and other women like you is to love yourself—fiercely. Nothing is as powerful as a woman who embraces herself, without apology.

YOU **DESERVE** TO FEEL **LOVED**.

Your sister, Annie, will help you embrace your inner power. Notice how she comes back every weekend from USC to visit home because she can tell that you're losing too much weight too quickly. She can tell that you're deeply depressed, and devoid of self-esteem. Read the book she gives you: *Reviving Ophelia*. Your sister is encouraging you to heal, and to eat again. Remember the warm feeling you'll feel in your belly as you realize you are loved. Don't feel guilty or selfish for wanting to feel more of that. You deserve to feel loved. Seek this feeling out with positive mentors. Thank your sister as much as you can for being almost like a mother to you. She cares deeply for you. Remember the power of a caring sisterhood—it can heal the deepest of wounds.

Stay grateful for her. Stay grateful for as much as you can. Gratitude is a surefire way to being more present in the moment. The more present you are in that moment, the less anxiety you'll feel. In fact, keep a gratitude journal if you'd like. List ten things you're grateful for each day. Eventually, you'll just start listing your gratitudes in your head.

Staying active in school will also help ease your anxiety, and allow you to feel moments of freedom. In fact, your obsession with student government is going to teach you one of the most important lessons in your life: that if you set your sights on a goal and work toward that goal longer than other people are willing to, you will get what you want. You're freshman VP now, and you'll hold offices every year until you become student body president senior year. You'll feel the power of demonstrating intention and persistence. No matter the challenges of your eating disorder and whatever the future brings, remember that you truly know how to persist.

"Keep Zen, and Try Again." You'll come up with that mantra in the future, and it'll get you through the turbulence of being a young woman, and an aspiring professional musician. Computers will crash, files will disappear, voices will crack, and songs will flop. Just keep going.

Remember when your third-grade teacher told you to take three deep breaths every time you feel anxiety? You're going to continue using that technique for decades to come. It's much like meditation.

When teachers and counselors tell you that they are proud of you, try to truly believe them. I know you have a hard time trusting that adults will appreciate who you are, but they will. Your doubt is something you're projecting onto others because you feel low about yourself. Some of these teachers and counselors really care about you. In fact, your sixth-grade art teacher is going to reach out to you when you're in your twenties, and she's going to tell you that she was worried about you because you seemed like a very depressed kid, and that she wanted so badly to help, but you were too shy and fragile to open up at that time. Depression is real, even among kids. So you're not being overly dramatic when you feel like you have chronic depression and anxiety.

Laugh as much as possible. Don't take yourself, and your appearance, too seriously. Life is beautiful—as are you—and you're just getting started.

Stay curious. Stay rebellious. Stay goofy. Keep being curious about vegetarians and artists. Keep listening to music, even if you're told it's distracting you from your studies. As a Los Angeles kid, you spend a lot of time in the car, and when you find yourself studying the drum patterns on Stevie Wonder's tracks, you're not spacing out. You are studying the music. And that little voice in you that says you're meant to be a singer? Have faith in that little voice. She knows you better than you think. Let that little voice keep getting louder. Don't let it keep quiet. She is going to lead you into songwriting, which will save you from anorexia, deep depression, and your inner monsters.

She'll tell you:

"You are enough. Just as you are."

Love,
MILCK

LAUGH AS MUCH AS POSSIBLE. DON'T TAKE YOURSELF, AND YOUR APPEARANCE, TOO SERIOUSLY. LIFE IS BEAUTIFUL—AS ARE YOU— AND YOU'RE JUST GETTING STARTED.

— MILCK

CHAPTER FOUR

BEYOND STRESS AND SADNESS

IT'S NORMAL TO FEEL stress. There are many different kinds of stress we experience over the course of a single day (or even over the course of hours or minutes). We can feel good stress, like when we're working out or finishing a huge project. We can feel less-good stress, which might pop up before a big test or a presentation or before a social event. It's also normal to feel sad. There can be sad days and sad weeks and, sometimes, sad months or years. We can have a string of bad luck, loss, or failure. We can find ourselves crying because of pain or illness or because we've lost something or someone we love.

But even though stress and sadness are a normal part of the human emotional experience, they can become too much. Anxiety is a nonstop pressure chamber of stress that presses down upon those who experience it, rendering them unable to do normal, everyday things for the fear of what might—or might not—happen. Depression, which can exist by itself or in conjunction with anxiety, brings a kind of crushing sadness and listlessness. It's beyond a sad day or week or month and can emerge with or without an incident to cause it.

Anxiety and depression make up two of the most common mental health challenges today. Better understanding how anxiety and depression work not only helps those who struggle with them but can also help those who don't to better navigate their own emotional hills and valleys.

RITUALS

by Libba Bray

(Night. A not-too-crowded plane, thirty-seven thousand feet in the air. Economy class. Find: A writer, "ME," reading a book under the artificial glow of the cabin light. To her left, the seatmate by the window snores softly under his blanket. ME seems slightly anxious. She chews at a fingernail while she reads. Then, suddenly . . .)

OCD: Hey!

ME (startles slightly)**:** Oh, hey. I didn't know you were on this flight.

OCD: Dude. I'm on every flight. Whatcha reading?

ME: Um, nothing.

OCD: Let me see.

ME: 'S just a book. No big.

OCD: Let. Me. *See.*

(Defeated, ME shows OCD the book.)

OCD: Dude. This looks awesome! How many pages in are you?

ME: Not far. Like, page fifty-one?

OCD: Hmmm.

ME (irritated)**:** What?

OCD: I feel weird about page forty-seven. Did you really read it thoroughly? No skimming, no cutsies?

ME (through gritted teeth)**:** Yes.

(OCD quirks an eyebrow.)

ME: I mean, I—I think so?

OCD: You think so.

(OCD drums fingers on the tray table in a specific rhythm, going from pinkie to thumb, over and over.)

OCD: Something's off.

ME: Nope. All goo—

OCD: Maybe you should go back to page forty-seven and read those last two paragraphs again. Just to be safe.

ME: C'mon, man. Please. I gotta finish a chunk of this book before I land. I can't stop to reread every page.

OCD: It's not *every page*. Just page forty-seven.

ME: I thought we were through with this.

OCD: We're on a plane. You know the drill. (stares)

ME (heavy sigh)**:** Fine.

(ME flips back in her book to page forty-seven. While she reads, OCD looks over ME's shoulder, giving her no peace.)

OCD: And don't forget to read the last word of every paragraph before you turn the page. And note the page numbers on both pages, left side, then right. And then the page number on the next page—

ME: For fuck's sake. Would you just let me . . . ?

(OCD bows in a Fine, Do-Your-Thing gesture of acquiescence, then

grabs the safety instruction chart from the seat back and begins
to memorize it. With a head shake, ME reads her book carefully,
noting the last word of every paragraph. She stops. Frowns.)

ME: Wait, two of the words are hyphenated, so how do I . . . ?

(OCD keeps eyes on the safety chart.)

OCD: Read the word before, too, and the word after. Just to be sure. (beat) There's
no way this pillow will keep us alive in the water. It's polyester. And fiberfill.
(whispers into the card) You. Are all. Marked. For. Death.

(The seatmate stirs for just a moment. ME whispers fiercely to OCD.)

ME: Can you knock it off-fay with the eath-day?

OCD: Whatevs.

(ME continues reading meticulously, as if she were studying a
religious text. OCD watches her. Squints.)

OCD: You know what? I think you should probably reread pages forty-eight, forty-
nine, and fifty. Just to be *aaaabsolutely* sure.

ME: Wait a minute! We had an agreement—just page forty-seven.

OCD: I didn't realize how bad things were! You want to be sure, don't you? Hey, can
I eat your peanuts?

(ME angrily tosses over tiny bag of airline peanuts.
Suddenly . . .)

ANXIETY: Did somebody say "peanuts"?

ME: Great. *Now* look who you woke up.

ANXIETY: I've been awake the whole time. You know we're a team.

(ANXIETY opens hoodie to reveal a T-shirt that reads: I'm with
OCD!)

ANXIETY: Anyway. Peanuts. Big old no! So much nope. Too risky. What if your throat closes up?

OCD: Good point. Excellent point.

ANXIETY: Thanks! (bites nails) Careful with the compliments, though. Makes me nervous. I'll feel like I can't live up to the hype. Like I'm just waiting to disappoint you. (staring, wide-eyed) I'm a fraud. Everyone knows it. I shouldn't even be going to this conference.

(ANXIETY breathes in shallow huffs.)

ANXIETY: I feel weird. Maybe there's peanut dust in the air? (looking around) Who did it? Which one of you ate the allergen sandwich? Which one of you is a *secret murderer*???

ME: You guys, we have literally been eating peanuts and peanut butter our entire lives. We. Are not. Allergic!

ANXIETY: Till *now*. What if that allergy is lying dormant, like a sleeper cell? I mean, anaphylactic shock at thirty-seven thousand feet would suuuuck so hard. And I never erased the *Xanadu* soundtrack from my iPhone. What if they play that at my funeral and the last thing people know about me is that I liked really terrible musicals? Oh my god. I can't breathe. Seriously, I can't breathe.

ME: Now *I* can't breathe. Shit. I am not having a panic attack on this plane, I am not having a panic attack on this plane, I am not—

ANXIETY: REACHING MAX FREAK-OUT LEVELS!!!

OCD: Let's do the thing, you know, where you rub your fingertips across your fingernails from nail bed to tip?

ME: I know what it is! I've been doing it for years, thanks.

OCD: It's a great self-soother. I like that one. Not too obvious.

(ME performs the fingertip ritual covertly. She begins to calm.)

ME: I just. Want. To read. My book. Can you guys go sit somewhere else? Look— here comes the flight attendant. Just . . . act cool for once, okay?

ANXIETY: But I'm not cool. I've never been cool. (beat) Order me a Pepsi?

OCD: Remember to wipe the top off first.

ME: They don't have Pepsi.

OCD: Why don't they have Pepsi?

ME: Do I stock the plane?

ANXIETY: Pretty sure there's an FAA report somewhere on the correlation between airlines that don't stock Pepsi and crash frequency. (whispers) We're on the Pepsi-less plane of death!

ME: I'll order you an apple juice. They give apple juice to toddlers. It's safe as houses.

ANXIETY: Houses aren't safe. They can catch on fire. Some are haunted. All those doors and windows and basements. (whispers) Terrifying.

ME: *Drink. Your. Apple. Juice.* I have work to do, okay?

(ME goes back to reading, but she's clearly laboring over the book now, examining every word.)

OCD: Hey. Did you count by sevens and threes when you got on the plane?

ME: Yeah.

OCD: It felt wrong.

ME: (beat) Shit. It did, didn't it?

OCD: Right? Do it again.

ME (slumps): Dude. I really, really have to read this book. I'm moderating a panel—

ANXIETY (singing softly): We are going to die. It will hurt a lot, *sha-la-la-la, sha-la-la-la,* I am sad that I never went to Paris, *sha-la-la-la, aha-la-la-la* . . .

OCD (steely): Do it. Again.

(ME folds her arms across her chest. She will not be bullied.)

ME: No.

ANXIETY (louder)**:** Going to die, going to die, we are going to going to die, die, die!

OCD: Come on. Just do it.

ME: Nope.

OCD: It's easier than fighting it.

ME (like a mantra)**:** You are figments of the overactive fear center of my brain. You are some internal drama I have created around integrating and accepting all my imperfect selves. You are my defense against feeling disappointment and anger and intense sadness. My feelings will not kill me. They will not kill anybody else. I am making a stand against your tyranny.

(ME stares down OCD and ANXIETY.)

ANXIETY (gasping)**:** Can't . . . breathe. Can't. Breeeeattthhhee . . .

(OCD mirrors ME's posture, arms folded across chest, mouth pulled into a taunting sneer.)

OCD: Sure. You can make a stand. Go ahead. I mean, the plane will probably crash and it'll be all your fault. But, ya know. Whatevs.

ME: We have been over this a million times. We don't keep the plane in the air with all our compulsive anxiety rituals. It's the pilot who keeps the plane safe. And the copilot. And physics.

OCD: Do you really want to test that theory now? Look around. (whispers) There are *children* on this plane.

(Defiant, ME slips on a pair of headphones and pulls up iTunes on her phone.)

ME: Ignoring you both. Putting on Arcade Fire.

(Beat. Then OCD leans in and lifts one headphone.)

OCD (whispers)**:** Child. Killer.

(ME rips the headphones off.)

ME (in quiet fury): Okay, you know what? Enough. Don't do this. This is why I stopped inviting you guys to parties.

ANXIETY: That's okay. I don't like parties. I always say something that I *think* is funny but is really just weird and gets an awkward smile and then I wake up at 3:00 a.m. going, "I am *such* an asshole."

OCD: Maybe you stopped inviting us places. But we found you. We always find you.

ME (sighs): I know. (beat, tired . . .) I'll do the ritual.

(ME looks up to the ceiling. We're not entirely sure what's going on inside her head or what she's saying, but her lips move in some mysterious incantation we cannot hear. She does it rapidly, seven times. Then three times. Then another seven. She repeats it until she seems satisfied. Her hands drop into her lap.)

ME: Fine. I did it. Now, please. Just let me read in peace.

OCD (cheery): Great! (OCD's grin fades to a frown.) You didn't accidentally count to six, did you?

ME: What do you take me for, an amateur?

OCD: And not four, either? You didn't accidentally end on a four?

ANXIETY: I really wish we hadn't found out that four is associated with bad luck in Chinese culture. Now, every time I see a four, instead of thinking, *That's, like, half a pizza! Yay!* I think, *You are a little one-legged stork number of death. Be gone, harbinger of numeric evil! I will have none of thee.*

ME: You think "thee" while you're anxiety tweaking?

ANXIETY (shrugs): My fucked-upness is Shakespearean. Yea, verily.

ME: LOL.

OCD: Total LOL.

ANXIETY: LOL! LOL! LOOOOL! (beat) LOL is a palindrome. (eyes widening) Can you think of three more palindromes? Quick! Before the plane crashes. What if it hits an animal shelter? *What if we kill puppies?*

OCD: I need you to count the page numbers again. One more time. Just to be sure. We don't want the oxygen masks to drop from the ceiling.

ANXIETY: But just in case, I read the safety manual from cover to cover, exactly three times.

OCD: Me too.

ME (growls)**:** You guys! At this rate, it'll take me years to read this book. Forget it. I'm not reading on this flight. Happy now?

ANXIETY (whispers)**:** *Puppies.*

OCD: I didn't say you couldn't read. Just, you know. Be vigilant. To avoid disaster. Life is so fragile. It hangs by a thread.

(There is only the hum of the plane's engines. ME stares up at the cone of fake glow coming from the panel above her seat.)

ANXIETY: Gee. It *is* fragile, isn't it? The threat of loss is terrifying. The fear of pain, of losing those you love. The enormity of all that messy life. All those decisions to make. Consequences to accept. No reassurances except the ones you invent to create meaning. (beat) How do humans manage? How do you cross the street or let your children out of your sight? (beat) I'm freaking out again.

(ANXIETY breathes into a paper bag, looks to OCD for help, and in turn, OCD turns to ME.)

OCD: Can you do that thing with your eyes? The one where you look up to the ceiling exactly three—or seven—times while picturing the face of Jesus? But NOT sad, dying Jesus—

(ANXIETY lowers the bag for a second.)

ANXIETY (holding breath)**:** Never Sad Jesus!

OCD: The Happy, I-Have-Already-Risen-Check-My-Awesome-Vacation-Worthy-Glow Jesus.

ME (surly)**:** Yeah. *Familiar* with Jesus, thanks.

OCD: Can you bite the edge of your tongue a few times? You won't really feel it—you've got a callus there from all the other times.

(ME breathes in and out. Deep, purposeful breaths, as if staving off a medical crisis. Then, in the sort of overly calm voice used by mothers trying to soothe children on the edge of a tantrum . . .)

ME: I think it's best if I just try to write for a while. That's calming, right? To be immersed in writing?

ANXIETY: Yeah. Immersed in writing. Good plan. I like this plan.

OCD: Me too.

ME: Great. Swell. See? We're all getting along. Only (checks watch) thirty minutes until we land. We can do this.

(ME takes out her laptop and launches a document. She begins typing but stops suddenly.)

ME: Crap.

OCD: What?

ME: Nothing. I just messed up a word.

OCD: You gotta erase the whole word, not just part of it.

ME: Yeah. I *know*.

ANXIETY: Why do we do that again?

ME (rote): Because if I only erase the part that's messed up, it's like I've killed off part of the word's "family." The other letters in the word will be lonely. They'll mourn the letters that "died." Better to just annihilate the whole word so nobody is left to suffer. You get it.

OCD: Totally get it.

ME (shaking her head): I cannot believe I am ascribing human qualities to random letter groupings.

OCD: Can't be helped. The minute you erase only part of the word, your brain imagines that little word family at the funeral of the letters they lost. The grief is overwhelming.

ANXIETY: My heart hurts just thinking about it. So sad for them. I really wish I had a Pepsi.

ME: Drink your apple juice.

(Sounds of slurping through a straw. ME stares out the window at the tiny dots of light on the ground far below the clouds. From up in the sky, the shiny, isolated pinpoints seem to bend toward each other, light seeking light, as if desperate for companionship in those vast fields of nighttime loneliness.)

ME: Why am I so afraid? (beat) Why do I have to be the vigilant one? The Catcher in the Rye? (rubbing her eyes) It's exhausting. I'm exhausted. I'd like to not be me for a while. I'd like to be somebody who can get into an elevator no problem or read a damn book on a plane or who doesn't think that if she takes the little shampoos from the hotel bathroom, she's committing a crime and she'll be punished for it.

ANXIETY: Never take the shampoos. It's a trap.

OCD: Dude, not now. Epic soliloquy on deck.

ME: I'd just like to be somebody free. Somebody . . . normal.

(This is the truest thing ME has said in ages. It empties her to admit it.)

OCD: Hey. *Heyyyy,* buddy . . .

ME: I know this is all in my head. It's my brain telling me these things. Inventing you guys so I'll feel safe. But why doesn't knowing that intellectually translate into my being able to make it stop?

(ME leans her head back against the seat.)

ANXIETY (whispers)**:** Lice.

(ME immediately moves her head forward. She is about as uncomfortable as a person can be. Her frustration boils over. She is near tears.)

ME: My brain is kind of a douche.

(ANXIETY places an awkward hand on ME's arm.)

ANXIETY: Not always. Sometimes your brain is pretty awesome.

ME: You're making excuses for it.

ANXIETY: I AM SO NOT! What about the times your brain wrote all those books and stories and songs? What about how your brain feels when you're singing and the music moves through you all free and warm? What about the way your brain sees the beauty in so much—a rosebud of light slowly opening above the city skyline because it's morning, and mornings always bloom fragrant with new hope? The fact that you see early morning light as a rosebud signals that you believe, fervently, in hope. The way you can look across a room and sense loneliness or joy or alienation, some other human wanting to reach out but frightened of all that vulnerability and rejection, just like you, but doing it anyway, just like you . . . That empathy? That sometimes too-electric connection to the universe? That's some good stuff, right?

ME (quietly)**:** Yeah. I suppose so. I'm just . . . sick of this shit.

ANXIETY (hurt)**:** Sick of us?

(ME doesn't answer.)

OCD (hurt)**:** Everybody's got something kinda weird about them. Something that helps them cope. Their own private survival strategy. This isn't so bad. Like, what if your weird thing was that you had a third boob and you could never find bras to fit and it was hard to wear your laptop bag 'cause you were all, "Ow. Third boobage"?

ME: Okaaay. That's . . . oddly specific. (beat) Seriously, how long has that particular scenario been in your—

OCD: The point is, nobody's perfect. And our imperfections, our weirdo oddities, can't be separated from our beauty. People are a mixed bag. What have you got against being a big old mixed bag of beautifully fucked-up humanness?

ME: I just wish my mixed bag didn't make me so anxious.

(OCD elbows ME playfully. Grins.)

OCD: Do you remember when this whole thing started?

(ANXIETY laughs weirdly and too loudly, chews straw like a rabbit.)

ME (nodding, grinning in spite of herself): I started blinking my eyes in Mrs. Baxter's class—

ANXIETY: HA! "Blinking my eyes." As opposed to blinking your butt cheeks? HAHAHAHAHA!

OCD: Yo, chill.

ME (giggles): Butt cheek OCD. Now that's a neurodiversity I can get behind.

OCD: Aw, slick! Butt Cheek OCD is our new band name. High-five me. (beat) Dude, don't leave me hanging.

(ME high-fives OCD.)

OCD: Remember how Mary Mintner caught you doing the blinking and asked you, all judgy-like, what you were doing?

ME: Mary Mintner stole my pet rock collection just to be mean. She was a bitch.

ANXIETY: Don't call her a bitch. We're on a plane.

ME AND OCD: She was a superbitch.

ANXIETY (quietly but intently): She really was.

OCD: Anyway. You were embarrassed, but you could . . . Not. Stop. Because you hadn't hit the right number of blinks yet? It just didn't feel right.

ME: Mmhmm. And I was all, "Uh . . . it's the lights. The lights are bothering my eyes."

OCD: And she was all, "So stop looking at the lights, dummy."

ME: (beat) I figured it was just a weird phase.

OCD: Awww, hell no. Not my girl. You in for the long haul. (beat) Seriously, did you read page forty-seven exactly right? I don't think so.

ANXIETY: WE ARE GONNA DIE! OH MY GOD, DO IT DO IT DO IT DO IT DO IT DO IT DO IT DO IT DO IT DO IT DO IT DO IT DO IT—

ME: OKAY!

```
(ME frantically grabs her book and flips to page forty-seven,
reading the whole page over, paying special attention to the
words at the end of each line.)
```

ME: I did it. (sighs) Man. You are *such assholes.*

OCD: But we're *your* assholes.

ME: Lucky me.

FLIGHT ATTENDANT'S VOICE: Please prepare for landing.

ME: Thank god.

OCD: Look out the window. There's the runway down below. So close.

ANXIETY: I feel better knowing we'll be on the ground soon. We can pee. And then I can get a Pepsi.

OCD: It'll be okay to eat peanuts again.

ANXIETY: There's no elevator we have to take, right? Tell me we don't have to take an elevator.

ME: I'll find us an escalator.

ANXIETY (sniffs)**:** I love you.

ME: Yeah, yeah.

OCD: No. You really get us. And we get you. Hug it out?

ME: Yeah, no. We're in public. Later.

(The flight attendant's voice fills the cabin, detached as a priest's delivering a rote benediction.)

OCD: Time for our landing ritual. You ready?

ANXIETY: You got this, right?

(OCD and ANXIETY look to ME like children in need of protection. ME gives them a wan smile.)

ME: Yeah. Yeah, I got this.

(While other passengers perform their own ministrations—putting up tray tables and powering off devices, ME has her eyes closed, lost in her rituals: a compulsive repetition that takes on the aura of a religious practice, something holy, a prayer not only for herself but for every lost soul out there trying to get by as best they can. And for just a moment, as the plane hovers above the earth, her small, quiet voice joins the hum of the engines, the whine of the wheels dropping, the murmuring of passengers as they snap phone photos through thick windows, trying in vain to freeze the moment in time, as if they are all part of the same glorious dream and no harm can come to anyone . . .)

ME: Forgiveness. Forgiveness. Forgiveness . .

THE FIVE PEOPLE YOU OVERHEAR WHEN DEPRESSED AT A VAN GOGH EXHIBIT

by Emery Lord

When I walk into the Van Gogh exhibit, I'm at depression level 4. This estimation is based on the chart doctors show to help you describe your physical pain, a zero to ten scale with corresponding smiley faces. I use it to approximate my mental health, too. Being at a 4 means I am the chartreuse smiley face: mouth a flat line, with the word "moderate" floating above it. In other words, I'm beginning to consistently not feel feelings.

So, no, I do not especially want to be at the Van Gogh exhibit. But then, I do not particularly want to be anywhere. And looking at paintings seems healthier than staring at nothing in my bedroom, vaguely wishing a small, specific asteroid would descend through the ceiling. Besides, going to the art museum is experimental, like pushing a bruise. Will I feel anything? Or will I, surrounded by famed artistry, feel a continual and pressing blankness?

The top floor of the museum is overcrowded, and the only thing that keeps me from retreating is a tidbit I recently read about Van Gogh—the speculation that he was a "migraineur." That's the word the article used. So stylized, so posh! Like the condition happened exclusively on a velvet chaise, one hand draped across his forehead. Not, say, groaning in a dark room while he increasingly feared his skull would split like dry bark. Not struggling to walk to the bathroom because of vertigo. Not calling off work again, all too aware that it sounds like an exaggeration.

In other words, I—fellow migraineur—am so hideously lonely for commiseration about my personal Venn diagram of art, mental health, and physical health that I dragged my level-4 depressed ass out in public.

Chronic migraines are not my only physical issue, and depression is not my only tango with mental illness, but I think they're the two that intersect the most. Getting knocked out by a migraine for a day or two can act as a tripwire for depression. And, if I get a daylong migraine while already depressed, that nexus can really make me wish to be excused from the dinner table of mortal existence.

That sounds dramatic—I know. It does to currently healthy me, too. But twelve hours deep into what feels like an icepick to the forehead, with emotions that will not show up long enough to feel hopeful that it will end soon? Well.

Beyond even that, the two conditions share a lot: hours spent at doctors' offices, medication trials and costs and side effects, the occasional spike in severity. Canceled plans. Frustrated crying at the setbacks and lost time. Hours spent in bed begging for sleep or, failing that, an asteroid. That kind of thing.

I guess I just want to know if Van Gogh knew what it's like.

The exhibit is called *Into the Undergrowth*, and my first stop is its namesake, Van Gogh's *Undergrowth with Two Figures*. The canvas shows the forest floor in flecks of pale green, swipes of saffron. Poplar trees run vertical, blue-violet and flushed-cheek pink. The horizon looms dark between the trees. In the center, two figures are painted with few details, but one appears to be wearing a dress, one a suit.

Van Gogh painted it less than a year before he shot himself.

I'm standing near a middle-aged man and his young daughter. He says to her, "This one, I like."

I like the painting, too, but I only know that from memory. The museum owns it, so I've seen it before, and I remember feeling curious about the focus. Is it the two figures, centered but imprecise? Or is it the forest floor, rendered with such color and detail? If it's the latter, why even include the people?

Squinting now, I try to read illness into Van Gogh's point of view. I want to see it in his brushstrokes, the way you can see it in my fiction. Not always—just glimmers. If you share a specific malady experience with another, I think you can spot it sometimes.

So I try to spot it. The figures seem solitary and drab in an otherwise lively forest-world. That feels familiar, at least?

It's a reach.

As I move around the crowded room, I can't help but overhear the many conversations happening entirely too close to me. From them, I confirm that people only tend to know about Vincent van Gogh what I previously knew: *Starry Night*, those ginger-bearded self-portraits, and the ear thing. Oh, and that he was, as an older man standing next to me by one of the *Bedroom at Arles* paintings puts it, "Pretty freakin' *unwell*."

People do not tend to know when I am pretty freakin' unwell. For a lot of reasons. I don't want anyone to feel uncomfortable or burdened or—often, I just don't want to talk about it. But also because, frankly, most of the wrestling matches between my health and me happen in a dark bedroom. (Although, shout-out to the many strangers who saw me stretched out on LaGuardia's floor during my last public migraine!) Usually, the sole spectator is my husband. That's another thing that depression and migraines have in common. Only he sees me at my unhidable worst, when I am too exhausted or too sick to pretend it's not really hard. Only he sees the frequency, the nuance. Otherwise, both beasts are near invisible unless I mention them.

I move toward a timeline of Van Gogh's life, large on a prominent stretch of wall. His birth, his major career moments, and his breakdowns. This is familiar to me. Not his personal details, per se, but the inclusion of "episodes" in the timeline of someone's life. It's like any other milestone—a birthday or graduation or promotion. The calendar in my memory lists all the times the pain scale went past 9.

Van Gogh's biographical info doesn't mention migraines. It turns out I can feel one feeling today, and that is grumpy disappointment.

Near me, one woman asks another, "Did you know about the brother? I didn't."

I didn't, either. She means Theo, Vincent van Gogh's brother, who appears in approximately every third item on the timeline. They shared a close bond, exchanging hundreds of letters over the years. They're buried side-by-side. When Vincent died,

Theo wrote to his wife, "It was he who fostered and nurtured whatever good there might be in me."

I admit, Theo's existence and devotion surprise me. The middle school art class version of Vincent van Gogh painted him as so extraordinarily . . . alone. A genius, to be sure! But *suffering*. Desperate. Mad! I mean, the *ear thing*.

And maybe all that is true. It's just not the whole painting.

"He *wanted* to be committed," an older lady beside me tells her friend. "Did you know that? Can you *imagine*?"

Yes. And yes. (*Self-Portrait at Level 9.5*.)

"I just don't get it. His life doesn't seem so bad," the friend muses.

I imagine all the portrait lamps craning to put a spotlight on me. I'd tap-dance for these ladies, singing like in the finale of *All That Jazz*: "That's not! How it . . . woooooooorks!" Standing there, I wonder—as I sometimes do—if people think of suicidal ideation as thoughts that are obviously sinister. If they assume the voice comes in a snake hiss or a demon's warped bass. Does it occur to them that it could sound like the friend who nudges you at a bad, crowded party and whispers, conspiratorially, "Hey, let's get out of here." Do these women consider how well you have to know yourself to see that moment for what it is and whisper back, "You are not my real friend."

The last comment I can stand to overhear comes from a man speaking to his son. He remarks how selfish suicide is.

Maybe he cannot think of another way to articulate the fundamental thing he wants his child to know: that this thing—this act—is tragic. But why did he go straight to selfishness, of all things? Here in this overcrowded exhibit, the anger overtakes me. It feels like hot poison in my core, spreading out to even the tiniest vein, up my neck, down my hands. I'm so mad that my fingertips tingle; I feel like I could zap this man with the pent-up energy like a ragey adult Matilda. *"Van Gogh was really sick!"* I want to yell at him. "Tell your kid that mental illness can be very hard, and how important health care and access are, how we have to talk about it."

I mean, honestly, what are all these people even *doing* here? Do they just *love* irises? Go to brunch! For god's sake, if you can still enjoy the taste of pancakes, eat them! I have lost access to that particular pleasure. And all pleasures. ALL I HAVE IS THIS ROOMFUL OF PAINTINGS AND IT'S NOT GOING GREAT.

HUMOR TAKES A LITTLE POWER AWAY FROM DEPRESSION AND MIGRAINES.

I fantasize cutting off my earlobe just to throw it at the boy's father.

"Sorry!" I would say, wild-eyed with blood dribbling down my neck. "Sometimes we *unwells* just can't resist!"

I'm so mad that I start laughing. Because I can feel something! Is it some kind of noxious hate smog, leaking out from my pores? Yes! Is it a deep resentment toward people who do not understand? Yes!

But it is *something*.

I am wrong in that moment. I am objectively, statistically wrong, and I know it even then. In a room that crowded, plenty understand very well, and some have certainly suffered more than I. Maybe even this very man has grappled with depression! Health—mental and physical—intersects with every other part of life. And when I'm healthy, I feel lucky that I've woven a support system and resources—treasured ropes that, together, make a fairly sturdy net. There are worse things than this head of mine, and we do okay with art and with a Theo or two.

That night, I settle back into bed with my laptop, hunting for more Van Gogh information. I watch video clips; I read some letters between Vincent and his brother. It's good that I am interested enough to do this, even if I am mostly journeying back into the 1800s as a pathetic grasp for commonality.

One thing I have learned from years of migraines is that I can try medicine and sometimes find comfort in distraction—a podcast at a low volume, a bath. But, usually, I just have to outlast them. It's been a useful lesson for depression.

Outlasting doesn't feel very noble, though. It mostly feels like being in bed.

Eventually, my husband comes upstairs and lies beside me.

"Verdict on the exhibit?" he asks.

"Liked the paintings; hated the people," I offer, and he laughs at my uncharacteristic meanness. Some nights, I can joke about how bad I feel. Humor takes a little power away from depression and migraines. They can hurt me, but I still take potshots, making little dings in their metal exteriors.

From my art expedition, I wanted camaraderie. I hoped to see the specific cross-section of mental illness and pain reflected on canvas. But maybe Van Gogh didn't even have migraines. Maybe he wasn't trying to convey his personal life through art at all. Maybe he was just trying to render wheat fields on canvas and get through the day. That's what I'm often trying to do, in a manner of speaking.

So I didn't get my kinship. I got a glimpse at *Undergrowth with Two Figures*. I got Theo. I got angry.

And I came home to someone who sees my whole painting, who stays beside me for every bullet point on my life's timeline.

He reaches for my hand.

Our bedsheets have a small pattern, swipes of pale blue. Outside the windows, trees run vertical, dark sky bleeding between them.

I do not wear a dress. He does not wear a suit.

But here in the undergrowth, there are two figures. Why would I focus on the forest floor, when I could look at that?

FIGHTING THE WAR ON THE HOME FRONT

For Zadie

by Clint Van Winkle

The other day, as I prepared dinner, my young daughter ran into the kitchen and tried to get my attention. Even though I heard her bare feet slapping the ceramic-tile floor and her little voice call out for me, I didn't react. My mind was somewhere else, fighting a war that I shouldn't be fighting anymore. Sometimes the past overtakes the present; it whispers doubt and despair into my ear. Sometimes this happens often. And while I don't know how much my daughter will know about my military service by the time she is old enough to read this, I am sure that somewhere along the way she will realize that her father is different from other parents. My combat experience left an indelible mark, a stain, really, on both of our lives.

I was a twenty-five-year-old Marine sergeant when my unit deployed to Iraq. I'd spent years training for the opportunity to fight an enemy. Whether it was reading books on tactics or conducting martial arts classes for my unit, my life up to that point had been spent studying war and honing my fighting skills. Knowing we were about to invade a country that had a sizable opposition force made me extremely happy. Most, if not all, of my unit felt exactly the way I did.

Marines are a unique assemblage of ruffians who take pride in being Marines. People don't usually join the Marine Corps to learn a trade or to get free college. People typically join because they want to fight: Marines want nothing more than a war. And that was about to come to fruition. What I didn't know was that those of us who survived combat would still have a price to pay.

Certain sights haunt me more than others. And these are the gruesome images that cause my mind to drift. These are the things that mentally pull me away from my family and friends.

We were a sandstorm of destruction rolling across Mesopotamia, a swarm of locusts devouring the land. Death was everywhere. Every breath we took seemed like a gift. Bloated bodies lined ancient roads like trash piles of flesh. They festered in the desert sun and became meals for packs of dogs. I stood in a vehicle that was painted red with the blood of US Marines. None had made it out alive. Those sights were from just the first few days of our combat deployment.

Sometime after the Battle of An Nasiriyah, which was one of the biggest fights of the initial invasion of Iraq, my unit came across a white passenger bus. The bus sat in the desert, a mere hundred yards off the blacktop road, and about a half mile away from a small village. Its tires were deflated, and the side that faced the road was pockmarked. It leaned toward us, like it had a secret it wanted to share. I pulled a disposable camera from my camouflaged CamelBak and snapped a photo. My mind did the same.

Marines got out of their vehicles. The infantry secured the perimeter. I waited in the turret of one of the amphibious assault vehicles (AAVs) I commanded, behind a .50-caliber machine gun and MK 19 grenade launcher. These instruments of death had already proven themselves in An Nasiriyah, and both stood ready for my command to spit out their venom again. Our unit inched closer, then stopped in front of the passenger bus. Pieces of cloth hung from the shattered windows and moved gently in the soft breeze. Something seemed off. I reached down and caressed my machine gun's butterfly trigger.

About a hundred people from the small village had gathered behind our convoy. They were clearly agitated. Some yelled and shook their fists in the air. Others appeared to be sobbing. I called over the radio to my Marines, told them to stay alert, and then traversed the AAV's turret so it faced the bus. I trained a pair of binoculars on the bus.

The pieces of cloth hanging from the windows were the clothes of innocent Iraqi women and children. Some of the children had been small babies still in their mother's arms. Some were toddlers, about the same age my daughter is now. All were dead, pulverized by gunfire. Their fathers would never get to hear those little bare feet slapping tiled floors again. Their little voices would never call out for anyone again. Iraqi soldiers had loaded the bus full of women and children and then used them as human shields. When a convoy of Marines approached the bus, the Iraqi soldiers began to shoot. The Marines returned fire and killed everybody on board. The Marines didn't have any way of knowing what they were doing, that the bus was full of civilians, or that they were being goaded into killing innocent people. They saw gunfire and reacted. US Marines are efficient killers, and that unit proved that fact.

Even though it was horrible to see, one of the images that really stuck with me about that incident was the bus's windshield wipers. They, along with a sole uniformed survivor, were the only things that made it through the shootout. The man lay in the desert injured; the windshield wipers swept uneasily across what was left of the windshield. I wanted somebody to turn off the wipers and to shoot the man who helped facilitate the bloodbath. We did neither. Instead, we loaded up and drove off. As we pulled away, the villagers closed in. They wanted to retrieve their dead. They wanted to exact revenge on the one Iraqi soldier who had survived. Whatever they did to that Iraqi soldier probably wasn't good.

The windshield wipers never stopped moving.

I wish I could say that was the worst thing I saw or did in Iraq, but it wasn't. There was still plenty of death to witness and cause. Dead children. Dead Marines. Dead dogs. Dead emotions. Iraq stole a piece of me. Fifteen years later, and I still find myself mentally traveling back to that Middle Eastern war zone. I think about war, write about war, and, at times, dream about war. The images are as vivid as the day I first saw them.

It has gotten dark for me, really dark. Panic attacks, insomnia, and depression have been constant companions. At first, I drank heavily, which only compounded my issues, so I stopped. After a few years of dealing with the war on my own, I was diagnosed with post-traumatic stress (PTS). While it has been called many things over the years—soldier's heart, shell shock, post-traumatic stress disorder (PTSD)—doctors recently concluded that PTS isn't a disorder but rather a natural reaction to unnatural events. War veterans don't have a monopoly on it, either. Trauma is trauma

> # TRAUMA
> ### IS TRAUMA NO MATTER WHERE IT IS EXPERIENCED.

no matter where it is experienced. And I experienced my fair share of trauma in Iraq. It oozed from my pores.

For years, I tried everything to forget what I saw, but nothing could erase the memories. But with the work I did inside myself, I realized and accepted that remembering is okay, too. The pain, the memory, and the carnage all deserve a spot in my brain. The war is a part of me, it has given me a voice, and it has molded my thinking. I am who I am because of it.

But I refuse to let the trauma define me. Instead of running from PTS, I own it. I might be a former US Marine who has to sleep with a light on, but I am not broken. Hardened by trauma, yes, but not broken.

There are still days that I feel as if I am teetering on the brink of insanity. There are still days that I find myself wading through the darkest regions of my brain, dredging up memories that are best left untouched. Still, I refuse to allow this to break me. I refuse to allow the depression to win. I am alive. I say it out loud. I remind myself that while life is filled with painful moments, it is mainly beautiful.

I am alive.

I live life one day at a time. Today is a good day. Tomorrow might not be. I have to get better and have to make sure that I continue to take the appropriate steps to recover from the trauma. My little blond-haired daughter deserves a father who lives in the present. So I meditate: inhale positive thoughts, exhale the negative. I try to focus on the beauty that surrounds me. Whatever it takes. I will not let Iraq win. I will not let that experience destroy my family or me.

I am alive, and that matters.

WAYS TO SAY "ANXIETY"

by Esmé Weijun Wang

The commonplace scourge of anxiety comes in many flavors, and yet these wildly various experiences are all described with the same single word. In seeking a more granular approach, I exclude anxiety-related words such as "phobia," which are more about context; rather, I'm searching for words and phrases that call out whichever flavor of anxiety is present.

Here are a few of the words and phrases I use to whittle down the umbrella term. These are, of course, terms for me and my experiences of anxiety; my hope is that people will adapt and adjust them as desired.

NERVOUS—a sensation normally felt in the solar plexus or the belly; a tight ache that is somewhat sour; sometimes called "butterflies in the stomach"; usually felt in anticipation of something, though the "something" may be either good or bad; easily mistaken for excitement, or vice versa

PANIC—marked by breathlessness, with the corresponding inability to take a deep breath; smothering; nausea; a need to escape

ADRENALIZED ANXIETY—all systems are "go" in preparation to defend from attack; senses are heightened; terror borne of the absolute knowledge that something horrifying is about to happen

WORRY—thought-driven; the mind chants: *What if what if what if*; can happen after social interactions, causing me to fret over everything I've said in the presence of others; feels expansive, endless, and boundless

ANXIETY ATTACK—resembles panic, with the same breathlessness, but lacks panic's sheer terror; a largely physical experience that can be mistaken for various kinds of illness, or vice versa

ADRENALINE DUMP—adrenaline is flooding through the body with no corresponding thoughts or cognition; body based, not mind based; similar to "adrenalized anxiety," but might not be accompanied by terror

PARALYTIC ANXIETY—a sense of being overwhelmed that makes life so complex that I can't do anything; decision-making seems impossible; a useful time for a friend to instruct me to do something specific

META-ANXIETY—anxiety about having anxiety ("I can't believe this is happening—what is wrong with me?"); can also be anxiety about having any other form of mental malady; always makes the psychiatric symptoms worse than they were originally

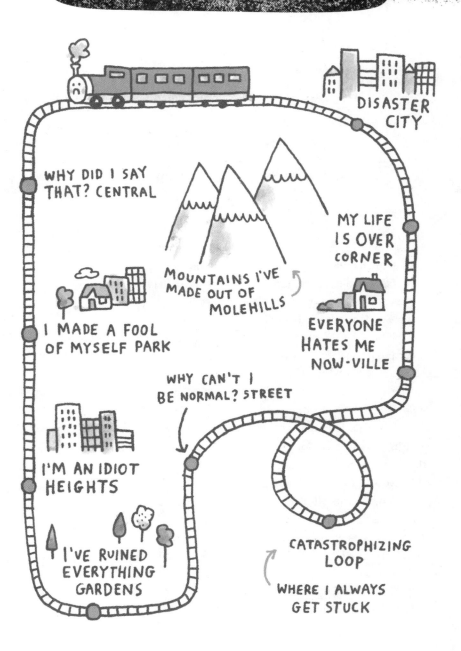

BLACK HOLE

by Victoria "V.E." Schwab

I sat down to write about the intersection of creativity and mental health.

    I sat down to draw a flowchart of circuitous thinking.

    I sat down to examine impostor syndrome, anxiety, perfectionism . . .

    I could have done any of those things.

    Instead, I'm writing about black holes.

    A black hole is a place where the gravitational pull is so strong that nothing escapes, and if you get too close or if you lose your footing, you get sucked in and down and down and down forever.

    One of my characters from *This Savage Song*, August Flynn, gets stuck inside his own head. His thoughts loop and tangle until, if left unchecked, they eventually spiral out of control. It seems like a minor character detail, considering that he's also a soul-eating monster, but for me, it was the trait that mattered most. It's the kernel of truth at the core of his design.

    I have always gotten stuck.

    A thought kicks off inside my head, and goes around and around until it has its own mass and gravity, a force strong enough that I can't seem to pull free. I started to think of this dangerous mental landscape as quicksand, but in truth, it's the opposite—because you *have* to pull yourself free. The less you fight against it—or the less you know how to fight against it—the deeper you sink.

    Will this be the time you can't break free?

    Will this be the time you lose yourself inside your own head?

Will this be the time gravity wins over hope, over desperation, over everything?

It's a mental loop. Not the kind that marks obsessive-compulsive disorder—there is no series or sequence of actions I need to fulfill, no obvious way to break the cycle. But it is, without question, obsessive.

I obsess over anything out of my control. I take a potential—and potentially innocuous—event, conversation, action, and obsess over its size, scope, every way in which it can go right or wrong depending on my actions and reactions. It's a game of chess played out with me on one side and the world on the other.

Nine times out of ten, the catalyst is something out of my direct control, but *adjacent* to it, close enough to the line to make the boundary feel porous. Close enough that I can convince myself of my ability, through meticulous action and sheer vigilance, to control it. The direction of a conversation, for instance, or the way others perceive me. You cannot, of course, dictate the thoughts and opinions of other people—that is a territory within their minds, not yours—but you can sure as hell obsess over it.

But my obsession wasn't always so broad or encompassing.

In the beginning, it was painfully specific.

It began with death.

Not a specific death—it wasn't formed by the sudden and jarring loss of a loved one—but rather the possibility of it.

Death is an inevitable condition, an event that no one can avoid indefinitely. And yet. And yet. And yet. It is a perfectly feasible focus for obsession, because it's possible to convince yourself that with enough vigilance, you can postpone it. With enough vigilance, you can steer those you love out of its path.

It wasn't my own death I leveled my energy on avoiding—I never held much fear in that respect—but that of my parents.

"Be careful."

Two words that drove—and continue to drive—my mother mad. Every time she would step off the curb. Every time she would chop vegetables. Every time she would round a corner in the car, or stumble on a stair, or cough on a bite of food.

"Be careful."

My mother wasn't ill.

But my father was.

My father was—and is—a type I diabetic; the disease forces him to straddle the precarious line between wellness and catastrophe. Things are better now, medically speaking, thanks to advances in insulin technology and monitoring, but when I was growing up, his health was a brittle thing. Every day, it was in jeopardy.

Having grown *up* in a world where he was not expected to grow *old*, my father, for his part, was incredibly fatalistic. He had come to an equanimity with death that I still do not possess. But if he would not take up the helm, I would.

By the age of eight, I had memorized the microexpressions that served as clues to his varying blood sugars (from 30 to over 300). By the age of ten, I could tell him his sugar with such frightening accuracy that he called me his personal glucose meter.

I was beginning to feel a dangerous level of control. Dangerous, because I knew it was a fallacy, knew that every victory was not a guarantee of those to come. And so vigilance became hypervigilance. Attention became obsession.

Once lodged in my mind, "Be careful" became *Be careful be careful . . .*

I don't know when the scale tipped. I only know that by twelve, I stopped sleeping. An obsession with my parents' health had evolved into a terror of losing them. Which, I reasoned, could only result from my failure to keep them alive.

The thoughts came for me at night.

I could fight them back during the day, when my parents were in front of me, alive and well, but the moment the lights went out, I fell under siege. While other kids my age stayed up with a flashlight and a book under the covers, I was lying in the dark, thinking about death until the thoughts became a weight and the weight became crushing.

While my parents slept, I lay perfectly still and studied their breathing through the walls of our house. My mother had a persistent cough that grew worse at night, and every sound was like gunfire, sudden and startling. My father was perpetually fragile, one wrong dose of insulin away from a rage or a coma, a bad blood sugar or death.

I now know the situation was not that clear-cut.

But a child's mind draws in black and white.

I grew up, and waited to outgrow this part of myself.

I waited and waited and waited and waited and waited and waited, and I am now thirty and my parents are still alive. While I have learned to keep the "be careful"s inside my head, I still think them. I still cringe when my mother coughs. I still panic when my father doesn't answer his phone. I am always one foot away from the black hole inside my head.

THERE IS A BLACK HOLE AT THE CENTER OF MY MIND.

I still get stuck.

No matter how vigilant I try to be, how wary of my mental footing, I can't seem to avoid that inevitable wayward step. It's only a matter of time before I slip, one leg plunging into the dark.

I have given up on avoiding that first misstep. The ground beneath my feet is full of pitfalls. I focus instead on stopping the descent, preventing myself from falling farther. I dedicate my attention to slowly, meticulously, hauling myself back onto solid ground.

And I do it by writing.

This is my lurid secret: I do not write because I love it. Certainly, the love is there, folded in somewhere alongside the discovery, the order, the completion of the act. It does not always parade as love—more often it is more a thrill of excitement, a wave of satisfaction—but it is there, and I have always seen it as a pleasant side effect rather than the purpose.

There is a black hole at the center of my mind.

It is always there.

But it is not all there is. It is a trap, a weak spot in the center of a wooden board, waiting hungrily for a misstep. But my mind is also brimming with other thoughts and ideas, ones that don't skew toward death, and loss, and the other thousand things out of my control.

Those ideas, they are my rope.

Rope is a fickle thing. Too much slack, and it gets tangled up. Too little, and it gets wrapped around your limbs and binds you. Rope has the potential to harm or to help, but to do either, it must be put to use.

I write because it makes use of the rope. Because it is the only way I've found to keep myself from plunging headlong into the dark. I write to stop myself from falling. I write to catch myself when I do. I write to have something to hold on to.

When I write, I dedicate a large portion of my mind, my attention—my sanity— to the task.

When I write, I have so much to keep in my head, there's little room for anything else.

When I write, the black hole feels small and far away, its pull little more than a faint drag (but still there, always there).

I am not always a good friend.

I am not always a compassionate daughter.

I am not always entirely "there" in my own life, let alone the lives of those around me.

But the simple fact is, I'm worse when I'm not writing.

It is a choice between distraction and despair.

The less I write, the more present I am. The more present I am, the more likely my thoughts are to run the familiar path to dark places.

There's a certain irony to the presence of that black hole. The way it warps the fabric of my mind has undoubtedly shaped my writing. After all, circuitous thinking helps me work through plots. The compulsive need to render and work through possible scenarios is a nightmare when those scenarios involve the deaths of everyone you love—but hey, it's great for world-building.

That is what I tell myself, but I know at this point I'm just looking for a silver lining. A light in the dark, when the truth is that black holes devour everything, including light.

"Idle hands are the devil's playthings," so the saying goes. But it's an idle mind I fear. There is a franticness to my pace. A desperation to my process. I am always working. Two stories waiting in the wings for every one onstage.

I am often asked how I write so many books, why I am *always* working on something—or two somethings, or three. It is because, through the carefully curated madness of creativity, I avoid the much darker places my mind is prone to wander.

Fiction is a safe harbor for circuitous thoughts. A place where it's not only acceptable but productive to wander down every path of possibility and plot every possible outcome.

Without stories filling my head, I am back in the dark, listening to my mother's cough, my father's shallow breath. The black hole yawns wide, and I feel myself slipping, threatening to fall.

I'M OVER STAYING SILENT ABOUT DEPRESSION

by Kristen Bell

When I was eighteen, my mom sat me down and said, "If there ever comes a time where you feel like a dark cloud is following you, you can get help. You can talk to me, talk to a therapist, talk to doctor. I want you to know that there are options."

I'm so thankful for her openness on this predominantly silent subject because later, when I was in college, that time did come. I felt plagued with a negative attitude and a sense that I was permanently in the shade. I'm normally such a bubbly, positive person, and all of a sudden I stopped feeling like myself.

There was no logical reason for me to feel this way. I was at New York University, I was paying my bills on time, I had friends and ambition—but for some reason, there was something intangible dragging me down. Luckily, thanks to my mom, I knew that help was out there—and to seek it without shame.

When you try to keep things hidden, they fester and ultimately end up revealing themselves in a far more destructive way than if you approach them with honesty. I didn't speak publicly about my struggles with mental health for the first fifteen years of my career. But now I'm at a point where I don't believe anything should be taboo. So here I am, talking to you about what I've experienced.

Here's the thing: For me, depression is not sadness. It's not having a bad day and needing a hug. It gave me a complete and utter sense of isolation and loneliness. Its debilitation was all-consuming, and it shut down my mental circuit board. I felt worthless, like I had nothing to offer, like I was a failure. Now, after seeking help, I can see that those thoughts, of course, couldn't have been more wrong. It's important for me to be candid about this so people in a similar situation can realize that they are *not* worthless and that they do have something to offer. We all do.

WE'RE ALL ON TEAM HUMAN.

There is such an extreme stigma about mental health issues, and I can't make heads or tails of why it exists. Anxiety and depression are impervious to accolades or achievements. Anyone can be affected, despite their level of success or their place on the food chain. In fact, there is a good chance you know someone who is struggling with it, since nearly 20 percent of American adults face some form of mental illness in their lifetime. So why aren't we talking about it?

Mental health check-ins should be as routine as going to the doctor or the dentist. After all, I'll see the doctor if I have the sniffles. If you tell a friend that you are sick, his first response is likely, "You should get that checked out by a doctor." Yet if you tell a friend you're feeling depressed, he will be scared or reluctant to give you that same advice. You know what? I'm over it.

It's a knee-jerk reaction to judge people when they're vulnerable. But there's nothing weak about struggling with mental illness. You're just having a harder time living in your brain than other people. And I don't want you to feel alone. You know what happens when I visit my doctor regarding my mental health? He listens. He doesn't downplay my feelings or immediately hand me a pill or tell me what to do. He talks to me about my *options*. Because when it comes to your brain, there are a lot of different ways to help yourself.

We're all on team human here, and let's be honest—it's not an easy team to be on. It's stressful and taxing and worrisome, but it's also fulfilling and beautiful and bright. In order for all of us to experience the full breadth of team human, we have to communicate. Talking about how you're feeling is the first step to helping yourself. Depression is a problem that actually has so many solutions. Let's work together to find those solutions for each other and cast some light on a dark situation.

This piece was previously published in Time.com.

DRIVER'S ED

by Mary Isabel

When I was in college, I was in a fender-bender on my way home from campus. I got T-boned by a driver rushing to lunch. It wasn't a big crash. I just had to wait a week for the part to fix the car. But when I got my car back from the garage, and found myself driving past the intersection where the wreck occurred, I gripped the steering wheel so tightly my hands trembled. My breath was uncontrollably fast, and my stomach lurched. I thought that I was going to be sick right there on the spot—vomit all over my dash. It wasn't until I realized how intently I was watching other drivers approach the stop sign that it occurred to me that I was in the same place where I'd been hit a week earlier. My body knew before my mind did: we've been here before, and it went badly for us.

I go back to that street when I need to remind myself how right it is that I don't move through life like other people. I don't always believe blinkers; I prefer to watch the wheels, judge the speed. I stay alert and focused, lest I miss my turn. I don't like traffic. I'm not sure I will ever completely trust other drivers. My rhythm is different, as is my road.

Before I turned two, my mom and brother and I moved into my uncle's house. His alcoholism and the way it unchained his willingness to hurt us saddled me with a complicated personality twitch. Growing up in an abusive home was like being in a car crash every day for eighteen years. Eventually, every interaction became anxiety provoking; it became impossible for me to trust other people. I developed post-traumatic stress disorder (PTSD).

My teachers saw me as introverted and shy with a dash of stubborn defiance. It's not their fault. Without context, the manifestations of my PTSD read falsely.

I remember my third-grade teacher trying to correct my inability to maintain eye contact. Poor woman. Her mantra was that eye contact was a measure of respect that showed people I valued them. She even said it showed I was trustworthy. Counting to "three Mississippi" was as long as I could ever manage to hold her gaze.

Neither of us knew I was doing the best I could.

I never had faith in the religion of eye contact anyway. My nightmare looked me right in the eyes. Over and over and over. "I'm going to throw you back in the street where I found you." I couldn't outrun my uncle's words; they always overtook me. "You're going to be so fat, you're going to leave a grease stain behind you when you walk." His desire to look right at me while he said these things made them true. He wanted to be sure they were taking root, burrowing into who I was. At the time, I was so focused on getting through each attack that I didn't take inventory on how I was being changed.

When other people noticed, they would sometimes ask my uncle what was up: "Why is she so frowny?" "Why is she quiet all the time?" "Does she ever talk?" He looked them right in the eyes when he said he didn't know. Those people asked me, too: "What's wrong, smiley?" "Are you talking to me or the floor?" It was years before I understood that the people who asked those questions didn't really want answers. Their words were thrown to make me duck into "normal." They were not trying to trace the source of my fears. Not really.

We all have things—and sometimes people—we are unable to look in the eye.

At the time, I thought I was lucky to get hit only with words, while my brother was made to listen to fists and feet. I didn't know that I, too, was being broken and put back together. I lost some emotional range in the process. Prolonged eye contact was among the things I have never recovered. Not yet anyway. I work on it every so often, with my counselor, and with an app on my phone. But I'm not worried about it. Eye contact is not a harbinger of decency. It's just a skill. It would be overstating the case to say that I ever "missed" it.

Growing up unafraid to say the wrong thing? I missed that. Allegedly, there were people who didn't practice words in their heads before they said them. They just opened up and were out with it. It sounded made up, but that's what I was told. Whatever that was called, that talking without practicing the sounds—without wringing out the words first, to make sure they wouldn't stain any moment—that would have been nice to try on as a kid, to feel it.

I wore that fearlessness eventually, but it was different. It was bigger than it needed to be. It wasn't an "in-my-own-skin" kind of easy; it was closer to armor. Secure in the way armor keeps both blades and sunlight at bay. Other people's words didn't hurt me anymore. Cruel or loving: they didn't touch me at all. It was as close to safe as I could create.

I missed being able to live in the moment, too.

The abuse took that away from me so early, I'm not even sure I remember what it was like. In many ways, I grew up in a town I created, in a story I wrote in my head, with imaginary people I know as well as anyone—maybe better. From early on, when things would get dicey, I would retreat into my mind and move imaginary characters through imaginary situations. Sometimes their situations mirrored my own. The adult male would get drunk and say awful things to them, but then the story would veer off into fantastical closure. They would confront their abuser, or be surrounded by helpful adults unafraid to act, or they would have some extraordinary moment that cured alcoholism, and ended abuse as I knew it. They were like me in a base way, but they had more skills, and more help at their disposal, than I did. Sometimes I was fully engaged in a fictional drama in my head while I was moving through my very real life.

When these real-life conversations would fall around me like so much heavy rain, I always had to come back to the moment I was standing in: pause the action I was imagining, pull myself out of the easy peace in my mind, and squeeze back into the right now. By the time I had fully arrived in the moment, I was soaked with other people's expectations. What to say was always blurry. I would shiver, practicing all the wrong words in my head, while people waited for me to say something.

I never lost my feel for what was really happening versus what I was imagining. I knew what was real, and what wasn't. It's just that what began as a place to go when my uncle was drunk wound up being way more interesting than my day-to-day life. It was fun to go imagining. I really liked my characters. Their lives were intriguing.

It felt good to step out of my skin—that of a pudgy, insecure, profoundly introverted girl—and into my mind, where I could feel what it was like to be, frankly, anyone.

At the beginning, and for the longest time, I imagined I was someone else. Somewhere along the way, though, I started being myself in the imagining. Other people changed, but I was me. That's when I started considering that the problem of my youth wasn't in me. Perhaps I didn't need to be "fixed" at all? Maybe it was my uncle's alcoholism and abuse that needed to change?

For a long time, I thought the imaginary world I created meant I was mentally ill. I didn't understand that it was my brain coming to rescue me. It's like my intellect and creativity arrived on the scene of an abusive moment, and said, "Hey, we got you. Let's get out of here." Creating people in my head gave me somewhere safe to go. Eventually, I put the people down on paper. Then I was able to tell people that I was busy writing. It became so much easier to explain what I was doing.

I hear some people don't have to work at staying in the moment. It seems like make-believe, but that's what I hear. Staying in the room is less work for me than it used to be. Like any skill I've sought to acquire, being present got easier with practice. I have learned how to ground myself in the moment, name the physical aspects of the space, touch them, remind myself that I don't need or want to leave just now, let safety settle over me.

When safety settles, my options become clearer. I can work on relearning any behavior that was taken from me if I choose to. Some of it, I am okay without. I remain convinced that eye contact is totally overrated. You know who can maintain excellent eye contact? Serial killers. If I never effortlessly go eyes-to-eyes with others? I can live with that.

The pieces that matter, though? I've worked to get them back. The talking that I was afraid of then is one of my greatest strengths now. I understand words differently. I'm careful with them. I know that the words I put on someone become part of who they are. And I have promised myself that no one I know will ever go through their life struggling to believe that they have worth because of something I said to them. It's one of a thousand ways by which I remind myself that I am not my uncle. I'm not him.

I don't sit around and wonder where the cycle of crashes and recovery ends. I know where it ends. It ends with me. Because that's what I choose.

THE PRETENDER

by Lisa Jakub

"Oh my god. You're that girl, right?"

It was a good question. Was I that girl? I didn't feel like that girl. But when I looked back, it was unmistakably me. It was my face, my hair, my smile on that poster. So I suppose I was that girl.

"Um. Yeah. I guess so."

Then the squealing would start.

This was repeated time and time again. In grocery stores and yoga studios and doctor's office waiting rooms.

But the question kept haunting me. Was I really that girl? I didn't know.

Here's what I knew: I had been an actor ever since I was four years old. Due to one of those random encounters that sounds like something out of a movie, a man approached my parents and me at a farmers' market in Toronto and asked if I wanted to be in a commercial his company was casting. I began my career before I started kindergarten.

It was a lightning strike. It wasn't planned or thought out. It wasn't something I worked toward or dreamed about or was deserving of. It could have happened to anyone. But it happened to me.

For the next eighteen years, I was an actor. It seemed normal. I didn't have pushy stage parents, but my career quickly turned into the focus of my life, like a kid who is good at flute or karate. But acting was not just an after-school activity. My formal education took a permanent back seat—I'd attend school when I wasn't working, but there

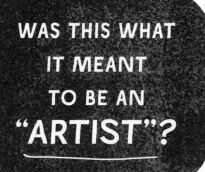

WAS THIS WHAT IT MEANT TO BE AN "ARTIST"?

wasn't much time when I wasn't working. I spent my life on sets in Dublin or Denver or Saskatchewan. Working on films like *Mrs. Doubtfire* and *Independence Day* and terrible TV movies in which I was blind or anorexic or experiencing General Teen Angst. When I was on set, I had tutors. We'd meet for three hours a day, usually in some cramped, smelly trailer, and I'd flip through social science textbooks and practice French conjugations while the crew finished lighting setups. I went back to Canada between film projects so I could attend my regular school, but I never stayed long before I got my next job. My school report card would list the number of days I was absent each term, and it was usually around seventy.

When I was eleven years old, I had my first panic attack. I was on the set of *Night Court*, and it was my first time working on a sitcom that was filmed in front of a live studio audience. It felt very different from a regular set. I was used to about sixty crew members standing around, but they all had jobs that required them to be watching the lighting or the wardrobe or the props. The live studio audience, however, was just there to watch the actors. They were there to watch *me*. An endless line of people filed into the studio and settled onto the metal bleachers as I felt my neck start to burn.

Suddenly, it was like someone removed all the air from the room. My vision got fuzzy and my hands went numb. My heart was pounding so hard I could taste it. I wondered if I was dying. But I had to get myself together and do my job, so I took a deep breath and said my lines. Eventually, the wave of anxiety faded, and I remember being surprised that I was still alive when it was all over.

And then it happened again. And again.

All through my teens, I battled anxiety and panic attacks. I had always been a sensitive kid, emotional and overly thoughtful. I worried obsessively and sometimes got sad for "no reason." I wondered if being so sensitive made me better at my job—was this what it meant to be an "artist"? But sometimes it all felt just too painful, and I cursed my tender soul.

For the most part, I liked my job. I got to travel and I made wonderful friends and loved being on set. We'd all show up at 4:30 a.m. and gather in front of the catering truck together, inhaling breakfast burritos before our long day of work that began at sunrise and continued long after sunset. It was intense but we were all in it together, working on this communal project. We were a family.

At least, we were a family for the next three months until the shoot wrapped and we all went our separate ways to work with a new family in a new place. It was a constant process—make a bond, be ripped apart, make a bond, be ripped apart. After each production finished, I'd get sick and curl up on the couch under a quilt for a couple of weeks. I'd try to go back to school, and to be a normal kid, but I felt lost—sometimes I was literally lost because I was so rarely at school that I could never remember how to get to the cafeteria. I didn't know where I belonged.

When I'd recover from my self-induced illness, I'd finally venture out of my house. But leaving home had its own challenges. I was never good at being recognized. It seemed like it would be great: people coming up to you out of nowhere and saying they like you. But to me, it felt like I was constantly being watched. Judged. Hunted. Peered at from behind doorframes and menus. And when I was doing some silly impersonation or had just eaten something green that was surely still in my teeth—basically, whenever it was going to be most uncomfortable for me—that's when someone would approach. An encounter would trigger my anxiety; my heart would pound and my vision would get fuzzy. Why was I so terrible at this? This was supposed to be the fun part of my job.

There was also the issue of what to say when I got recognized. People were generally pretty nice, but everyone asked the same questions over and over again:

"Was the movie fun to film?"

"What was Robin Williams like?"

"Did you keep in touch with anyone from the movie?"

"Was the movie fun to film?"

"What was Robin Williams like?"

"Did you keep in touch with anyone from the movie?"

I understood why they asked those questions, but I wanted to explain that there were lots of other things we could talk about, including:

"I rescued a dog!"

"I like to knit, but I can only knit flat things!"

"I sleepwalk!"

And I wanted to ask *them* a million things, too:

"What's your favorite book?"

"Have you ever had your heart broken?"

"Do you like turtles?"

There were so many things we could talk about. But they only saw me as this one thing—and this one thing was kind of weird.

It was in those moments when I realized that even though being an actor was normal for me, my life was not normal. I was not normal. I was something to be stared at. I didn't know where I would ever fit in.

So I started getting anxious about going out. Really anxious. It developed into agoraphobia, which, for those of us who get panic attacks, means the fear of being in a place where we can't easily escape if we feel panicky. I always needed to have my back to a wall. I needed to know where the door was. I needed to know I could bolt at any time. Sometimes just thinking about leaving my house and being around strangers would make me hyperventilate.

I dreamed of being a regular girl. I wanted to blend in and be completely unre-markable. But being a regular girl was not going to happen. I continued to travel to work on films. Eventually, administrators at my high school got so annoyed by my frequent absences, they said I was not a good fit for the school and asked me to not come back. Weirdo status: confirmed.

There were two major pieces of myself I felt like I needed to hide from the world: this weird actor life and an embarrassing panic disorder. I was ashamed because it seemed like everyone else had this life thing figured out. Everybody else seemed cool and happy-go-lucky. They got a little bit stressed, but they shook it off. They laughed easily with friends in the food court. What was wrong with me? I felt everything too much. I'd lie on the floor in my closet and obsess about why I was so sensitive.

When I was twenty-two, I decided to leave Los Angeles and retire from the film industry. My job had been great for a while, but the focus on superficial things, the competition, and the lack of privacy was just not a combination I wanted long term. It didn't feel like an authentic life for me. I wasn't sure what my true path looked like, but I knew I needed to live honestly if I had any hope of happiness. I didn't know who the real me was, but I knew she wasn't some Hollywood ingenue.

Even though everyone told me I was crazy to give up acting, I moved to Virginia, got my GED, and went to college. I'd hoped that my anxiety wouldn't follow me across the country, but when I arrived in my new life, it was still there, sitting on my shoulders and being a jerk. So I found a therapist and tried to figure out who I was beneath the actor. I started to really look at the thoughts that bounced around in my brain. I stopped running away from myself and took some power back from the negative self-talk that had dominated my mind for years.

It took me a long time, but I finally understood that all the things I felt I needed to hide were actually my superpowers. My sensitivity was something to be proud of. The fact that I feel things so deeply means I'm compassionate. I care. I'm engaged and alive and invested in the world. My unusual history gave me a unique perspective to share, and it made me who I am. When I learned to accept the things that I was ashamed of and worked with them instead of constantly fighting against them—I could do anything.

After I graduated from college, I tried out different jobs: I did communications for a nonprofit, I designed websites, I was a radio DJ. For one reason or another, I failed at each one. I struggled and then I picked myself back up and tried something else. All those experiences taught me that I'm far more resilient than I ever knew. I might be sensitive and emotional, but I am also strong and courageous and determined to live in a meaningful way. I can be all those things at the same time.

And then I found writing. And I found my heart. I found my voice and I found myself. I learned how to write through my anxiety, how to put my truth and my panic on the page and release them together.

I learned breathing techniques that helped when I felt like there was no more air in the room. I started practicing yoga because yoga teaches us to accept ourselves however we show up *today*. My old life was about constant striving, always barreling on to the next thing, the more impressive achievement. Yoga taught me to pause and show gratitude for this moment right here. It taught me how to find contentment within myself—my perfectly imperfect self.

Acceptance was the first step. Loving my anxious self was the basis of making some changes that made my life easier. Anxiety is just one part of me, along with the fact that I'm a devoted friend and a good cook and I buy multiple copies of my favorite books because I love to give them away. I embrace my weird now. I'm not ashamed of who I am. When I started asking for help when I needed it, I learned there is nothing weak about doing that. I realize now that it is incredibly brave to admit when my anxiety is more than I can handle by myself.

I still have anxiety sometimes, but I now have tools to help take my power back. I have compassion for myself when I'm having a hard time. I know that I can ride this difficult wave of emotion, and I'll be okay.

I'm done pretending.

COMPASSION TRAINING:
METTA MEDITATION

by Lisa Jakub

Metta, or loving kindness, meditation is my favorite way to calm down and feel a little more compassion for myself and others. First step: get comfortable. Sit on a chair or the couch or the floor. Lie down on the bed or on the coffee table. This is going to be challenging enough without forcing your body into some uncomfortable position. If you are on the floor, try sitting on the edge of a cushion or blanket, so that your hips are higher than your knees.

Breathe naturally and repeat the phrases (out loud or in your head):

```
May I be well.
May I be safe.
May I be happy.
May I be healthy.
May I live with ease.
```

Now insert the name of someone you love. And, yes, of course pets count.

```
May ____ be well.
May ____ be safe.
May ____ be happy.
May ____ be healthy.
May ____ live with ease.
```

Insert the name of someone you don't really have any feelings about. Like maybe your mail carrier.

```
May ____ be well.
May ____ be safe.
May ____ be happy.
May ____ be healthy.
May ____ live with ease.
```

Now insert the name of someone you have a . . . complicated relationship with. Someone with whom things are just plain difficult. The mere mention of this person brings up not-so-flattering feelings in your heart. It's okay—you don't have to tell anyone whom you chose to focus on here.

```
May ____ be well.
May ____ be safe.
May ____ be happy.
May ____ be healthy.
May ____ live with ease.
```

If that last exercise stresses you out, make sure you circle back to yourself again, because right now you are the one suffering. And remember that dealing with family is super high-level spiritual work.

```
May I be well.
May I be safe.
May I be happy.
May I be healthy.
May I live with ease.
```

The last step is to open up all this loving kindness to the wider world:

```
May all beings be well.
May all beings be safe.
May all beings be happy.
May all beings be healthy.
May all beings live with ease.
```

If you are trying to focus on all this lovely compassion but find yourself obsessing about that mean thing your friend said three months ago, that's totally okay. That's normal. When you have those thoughts, just come back to focus on your breath and the words. Don't beat yourself up. Don't decide that you suck at meditation and should stop. Just bring your attention back. Those random thoughts are like clouds on a windy day. Let them come and go. You're bigger than the clouds; you're the sky.

There are also many app options for meditation, such as Headspace, Mindfulness, Calm, and my favorite, Insight Timer. The latter offers guided meditations, music, ambient noise, and bells. It tracks your meditation sessions and offers milestones and cool graphs to keep you motivated. Try to get quiet for just a couple of minutes every day. For me, that was the tiny change that changed everything.

CHAPTER FIVE

TO BE
OKAY

OUR MENTAL HEALTH IS part of us from the moment we're born until we die. It helps shape who we are, whether or not we struggle with mental illness personally.

Self-awareness, through being conscious of our thought patterns and our cognitive habits, sets us on a path toward mental wellness. It also helps us practice empathy toward the people around us.

Key components of any discussion of mental health are the ways we manage our wellness, the ways we confront challenges, and the ways that we can come to accept what it means to be "okay." "Okay" isn't flawless, but it signals trying. "Okay" isn't a cure, but it's a measuring stick. "Okay" isn't perfect, but no one is.

Here's to the power of being "okay."

CODA

by Meredith Russo

A friend shifts between dragging and easing me out from under my blankets and into his car. I sit quietly as he drives, a bug-out bag of mostly books and hoodies in my lap, my mind rattling like a busted toy while once familiar streetlights streak by, suddenly alien and imposing. We arrive at the hospital after midnight, and it's quiet. Even though this is meant to be therapeutic, I take it as an insult that the world should be so serene when I am losing my ability to trust that it's even real. My friend sits with me for hours while we wait for the intake nurse, and he holds my hand through the nurse's weighing, poking, and questionnaires. I'm distant and faded enough that when the nurse asks if I have had "the surgery," I don't even think to be offended. There is a certain point where if everything hurts, then nothing hurts.

The nurse asks why I'm here. I explain that I've been hearing telephones, whispered voices, people outside windows. I explain that I have become certain everyone around me wants to hurt me. I explain that I spend long stretches of every day numb and almost outside my own body, that this has characterized my mind for most of my life to some degree, though it has recently gotten worse. For some reason, I believe this calm, easy professional will assure me this is normal, that everyone feels this way, that I am just under stress and my loved ones are fussing over nothing. His eyes still widen, because this *isn't* normal. People *aren't* supposed to feel this way, and, it turns out, I need help.

I get the impression that intake is finished when the nurse leaves, but my friend and I wait another hour, which means either they don't know what to do with my trans body or I'm unwell enough to merit serious concern. When he comes back with another nurse, I *think* they both look nervous, but it has become difficult to read human emotions, or my own, or to recognize any thoughts or words as human. The nurses tell me they had some trouble finding a bed for me because of my "situation." It had not occurred to me that I might be housed with men, but in a flame-burst second that fear rushes through. It is followed by unwanted, metallic memories of a night locked in a dark, cold room with strange men, and their threats, and their *promises*. I see beyond even the intake nurse's concern that now, in this moment, I am deeply, profoundly not well.

I get a room to myself, though. This is the only time being transgender has ever worked in my favor.

The doctor, who calls me by my dead name even after I ask her to stop, says I have bipolar disorder. She says it should have been diagnosed when I was a teenager and I went off the farm on almost every attention deficit hyperactivity disorder (ADHD) medication they tried, and that the combination of ADHD medication and nontraditional antidepressants I've taken for most of my adult life have kept me constantly hypomanic. This explains the low-key psychotic breaks I have experienced as I've gotten older. She says it's impressive I've made it this far. I don't tell her about the botched suicide attempts and near misses.

The doctor writes a prescription for a mood stabilizer and what she calls an atypical antipsychotic. I return to my room and lie down, not sleepy but not interested in speaking to other human beings.

The food is surprisingly good. I sit by myself and read. I might get released sooner if I smile and socialize, if I put real effort into normalcy, but this *is* normal for me. It's been a day since I last shaved, I don't have makeup, and I doubt being treated like a man will do anything to make me feel better. Besides, I'm cheating on my diet with a second brownie, and what's more normal than that?

. . .

I awake to find a line of patients outside my room near the nurse's station and join them, though I am careful to keep my shoulders hunched and my face turned, to prevent others from noticing I am a person with breasts and a beard. When my turn finally comes, the nurses refer to me by my dead name and masculine pronouns after I ask them to stop, or to at least lower their voices so other patients can't hear. They act confused about my hormones even though they were prescribed by a doctor. Once again, I am too tired to care much. They eventually track down my medications. I ask if I can have access to the electric shaver I put in my bag, explaining to these health-care professionals what gender dysphoria is, how it affects me, and that I would be happy to shave out here where they can see. I know for a fact, because it has been explained to me, that this is the ward for patients who don't present an immediate threat to themselves or others, that I am here, in this wing, precisely because nobody thinks I will do something like suddenly explode and try to kill myself with a pink electric trimmer from Walgreens.

And, really, how could I? But I get the impression that laying out the mechanical impossibility of the act, thus demonstrating how deeply I've considered it, won't do me any favors.

They refuse. I don't press the point, but when I retreat to my room again I *do* make a point of ignoring their insistence that I come out and participate in activities. Eventually, a nurse comes in with a clipboard and a form full of questions about my mental state. Am I hallucinating? I don't know. How would I know? Do I think anyone is out to get me? Yes, I certainly do feel that way, but it's a feeling based in reality, so I say that I'm not sure.

And, finally: Do I want to kill myself? Well, *yes*. I lied during intake, but I have thought about ending my life every day since I was fourteen, and circumstances aren't helping. I haven't grown a beard since I went full time almost a year prior, and every time I feel it on my chin and cheeks, I am revolted. The idea of what I will look like, what my body will feel like after a week of this, makes me want to scream and beat my head against a wall. Yes, I do, because everyone I care about knows I am in a mental hospital and this fact is embarrassing and I want it to not be true. Yes, because there are problems in my life transitioning couldn't fix, though it fixed many, and I doubt medication and talk therapy will do much more. But these all seem like perfectly reasonable feelings to me, and they're asking about *symptoms*, so I check the box for the lowest possible level of suicidality.

I will learn later that I'm not as tricky as I think I am, and that I fooled no one.

I finally get bored enough to leave my room, only to find a cop on the ward. He is tall and broad and flinty eyed, and I can barely look at him without remembering stripping naked, being asked if my breasts are real, and distant laughter. It occurs to me that this isn't his fault, that it might take a tremendous amount of strength for a man in his profession to admit that he needs help, that in here at least he doesn't have power over me. But then I overhear him talking to two younger women about freemasonry, and how a freemason's reverence for women stems from an understanding of women's utility, as if it's noble to admit you respect women because *somebody* has to fold your clothes and cook and take care of your children. I stay on the opposite end of the rec room, safely nestled in a cocoon of blankets and juice cups (we could hurt ourselves with the straws on juice boxes, you see), with my nose jammed safely into my book.

An hour later the sound of wood groaning across tile grabs my attention. I look up to see a short, muscular girl with a flower tattoo running up the side of her exposed midriff and her hair in a messy bun dragging a chair to my corner. She smiles and waves and I close my book, feeling a mixture of dread and excitement. She tells me she just got out of jail for buying pills from an undercover cop, and it turns out this wing doubles as a rehab center. She thinks my hair looks pretty and asks if I would let her braid it. Nobody has braided my hair before. Nobody has ever even offered to teach me. We sit with our legs crossed and watch that movie about the journalist in Mississippi during the sixties, and for a moment I consider telling my new friend that the same woman who published the book this movie is based on heads up the imprint publishing my debut novel. But it is maybe not the best idea for that information to spread. There are people waiting outside this hospital who will use anything they can find to hurt a trans woman, and they could have a field day with the knowledge that I've had a psychotic break.

Still, she makes me laugh. Her stories are outrageous and her fingers are deft, and the warm feeling in my neck as she plays with my hair reminds me that we really are a communal species, that we're no more equipped to stand apart from each other than chimpanzees or bonobos are. She slaps my shoulder and tells me to go look. I stand, and the cop turns his gaze to me. He squints and cocks his head now that my hair isn't framing my face, and I try to hurry past because just like that—just like that—all my feelings of warmth and safety have evaporated.

"What *are* you?" he says.

"I'm not sure what you mean," I say, my jaw clenched so hard I'm afraid I might hurt my teeth.

"She's a girl, idiot," my new friend says. My gaze snaps to her and she rolls her eyes, and I can't help smiling as I return to my room to check out my new look.

I spend the day coloring with other women, chatting about nothing in particular, all of us pointedly not discussing why we're here. The thought of playing with a coloring book as an adult was hard to swallow at first, but it really is relaxing, and I'm in a race with my new friend to color the most punk-rock mandala possible. A phone rings in the hall, but the other women don't seem to hear it. They give me strange looks when I mention that it's ringing, and then my forehead is pressed to the table and I am sobbing.

The antipsychotic is huge and hard to swallow. I sit with my new friends and read the side effects and health information, but it's hard to make out the words. I get stuck on a sentence near the bottom of the page and my eyes are h e a v y, a n d . . .

I wake up in my bed with no idea how I got there. The nurses, who use my dead name even though I ask them not to and continue to refer to me with masculine pronouns despite the distress this clearly causes me, say I slept for eleven hours. I feel like I could sleep for eleven more. I ask for my electric shaver, again calmly explaining my situation, and again I am told no. I take my medication (of course there is confusion with the hormones again, because this is a new rotation and I am always the first trans person everyone has met), retreat to my room, and wrap one of my bandanas around my face like I'm a bandit from a western. I get odd looks when I arrive for breakfast, but at least they're not looking at the awful hair sprouting from my face.

After breakfast, a nurse with the same form as yesterday finds me in the rec room. Just like yesterday, I answer that I'm not hallucinating, I'm fine besides feeling kind of generally upset, but then I get to the suicidal ideation section and instead of putting a one I put a two, followed by a note: *I am a trans woman, and you are psychiatric professionals, and you should know how to deal with this. My mental condition will continue to deteriorate so long as I am made to grow a beard.*

The day is uneventful. I feel lethargic and half asleep. The therapist, who uses my dead name despite my protests, explains that this is what life without mania is like. I'm not sure I like it. Another nurse does a class on how quantum mechanics is magic and if you want something badly enough, the universe will give it to you. This seems like an irresponsible thing to say to people with an already tenuous grip on reality, but I stay quiet.

I enter a three for suicidal ideation and repeat my note from yesterday. I've grown enough hair now that I can't take my bandana off without feeling profoundly sick, and when I touch my face, my hand feels like it's burning. Nobody has called. Nobody has visited. I understand that people are busy, and I wouldn't want anyone in my life to see me the way I look right now, but it still hurts. I try not to dwell on it. The day is uneventful and quiet. Everything is uneventful and quiet here. I take two naps.

The next day, I enter a four for suicidal ideation and repeat my note. I am torn between bored, sedated peace and gut-wrenching discomfort every time I catch my reflection in a doorknob. Somebody finds an old game of Monopoly in a cabinet beneath the television.

I have never enjoyed Monopoly more, which is to say that I'm actually enjoying it. Perhaps sedation is the key to keeping a game from descending into a screaming match.

As we put the game away, a nurse comes in and speaks with a young man in recovery from alcoholism—and possibly something else (I haven't asked)—about a drug that might help him. He suddenly looks haunted and he drags his feet as he returns to the table. I don't want to pry—it's an unspoken rule here that you don't pry—but he offers his concerns up anyway. He wants to get better, he really does, he's destroyed his relationship with his family, he's out of money, he's lost job after job, and he tried the twelve-step program on its own and it didn't work. But one of the possible side effects of this drug that might save his life is gynecomastia.

He doesn't use the scientific name, of course. "I don't want to grow boobs. Can you imagine?" But then he remembers who he's talking to and his cheeks flush. I smile because, believe it or not, I can sympathize with a person feeling uncomfortable with unwanted secondary sex characteristics. I explain to him about trans men, and that many of them have larger chests than he could ever have but with a binder, nobody would ever know. I give him some names of guys to look up, guys to reaffirm that you can still be masculine no matter what shape your body is, and most of his anxiety melts away. He goes back to talk to the nurse, and I don't hear what he's saying, but I see him nod.

Braid friend shows me photos of her niece. I have not seen my son in days. I break down crying and she shields me so the nurses can't see and misinterpret it as a symptom.

Sleep. Wake. Dead name, masculine pronouns. Suicidal ideation, five. Sleep. Wake. Dead name, masculine pronouns. Suicidal ideation, six. I stop leaving my room. The therapist, who persists in using my dead name, stops by on her daily visit, asks what's wrong, says I seemed like I was getting better. I tell her I'm done explaining this to people, that I've been explaining it every morning to the nurses at the desk and I've written the explanation every day and I'm done. She tells me it won't look good if I don't come out and participate. I wrap a blanket around myself and start a new book. Sleep. Wake. A knock at my door. I look up ready to snap at the therapist again and find instead a severe older woman in a gray pantsuit and floral scarf. She asks if she can have a moment. I follow her into the hall and we talk as we walk away from the rec room.

My treatment thus far has been against hospital policy, and the staff has been reprimanded, she tells me. I make a note not to smile next time I see them. She apologizes for my treatment. She uses my name and feminine pronouns. She tells me my shaver is behind the desk and I'm welcome to use it so long as I keep my room door wide open, but only for my face. She reminds me that cis women have to deal with hairy armpits and legs in here and I'm no different from them. I laugh, and for the first time since our talk began, she cracks a small smile.

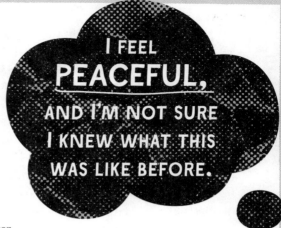

I FEEL **PEACEFUL**, AND I'M NOT SURE I KNEW WHAT THIS WAS LIKE BEFORE.

No song has ever sounded sweeter than the buzz of my shaver. It doesn't get everything. My chin still scratches a little and there's a shadow on my cheeks when I check the mirror, but it's something, and it's the best I could expect in this circumstance, so it's easier to accept. I dump the hair down the drain and hand my salvation back to the nurse, who looks thoroughly chastened and uses my correct name and feminine pronouns. I head to the rec room and my braid friend wolf whistles. I grin and wiggle my hips before sitting down.

Now that my dysphoria is under control, I take inventory and realize that I actually do feel okay. I haven't hallucinated in days. Outside of expecting transphobia from most cis people and not being disappointed, I have not once assumed anyone was out to get me. Even the cop seems to me now a sad and lonely man, lost in the widening gulf between his infirmity and the requirements of masculinity. I can talk to him without turning into a twitching, nervous mess. I have gained a little weight, which is maybe not ideal but, considering what weight loss usually precipitates in my life, is probably a good sign. I consider this as I dangle upside down from one of the rec room chairs, nibbling at a cracker and half watching some show about renovating houses. I feel peaceful, and I'm not sure I knew what this was like before.

Braid friend, coloring book friend, high school friend, boob anxiety friend, even cop friend surround me and hug me once I'm done packing my things. Some of them cry. I certainly do. They give me my shoes and I put them on in the rec room, marveling that it's been a week since I wore them, that something as simple as footwear can mark the distinction between the well and the unwell. A nurse leads me off the ward, down halls I don't recognize, and into the lobby, where I sign some papers. The quiet that offended my rattled mind only a week before is nice now, clean and safe like a fall breeze. I charge my phone, ask a friend for a ride, respond to a few people wishing me well, and step outside.

The sun has just begun to set, and banks of fog roll down from the mountains, through the trees, to crawl along the whispering fields just past the edge of the parking lot. I take my shoes off and stand on the earth, breathing and listening. I fold my legs beneath me and run my fingers through the grass. In my stillness I notice a family of deer edging through the shadows in the tree line, quietly watching me. Because I make no sudden moves, they venture out, their hooves as quiet as thoughts, and they come almost close enough to touch.

This is not the end of my recovery. There is no end to recovery, honestly, and realizing that is itself part of learning to heal. But I will look back at this moment, at this quiet coda and the week before it, as the point where I began to heal in earnest.

TEARING FEELINGS APART
BY YUMI SAKUGAWA

WHAT IF

INSTEAD OF DROWNING

IN YOUR SELF-HATING THOUGHTS

YOU SPREAD THEM APART

LIKE COTTON CANDY

AND THEN THE LETTERS THEMSELVES

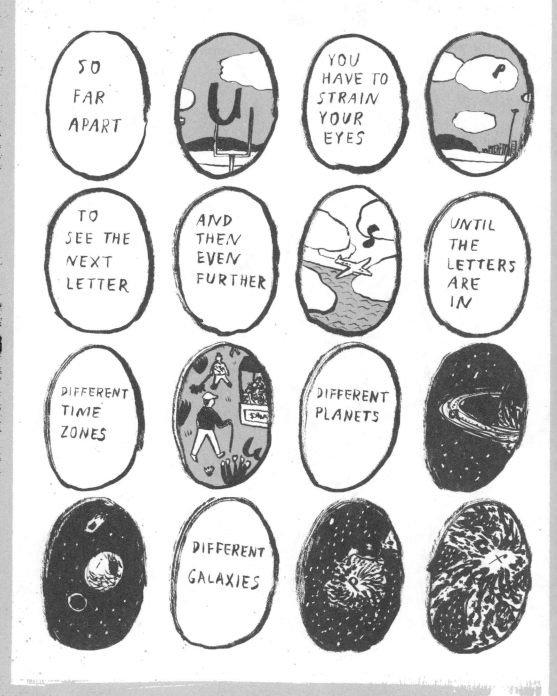

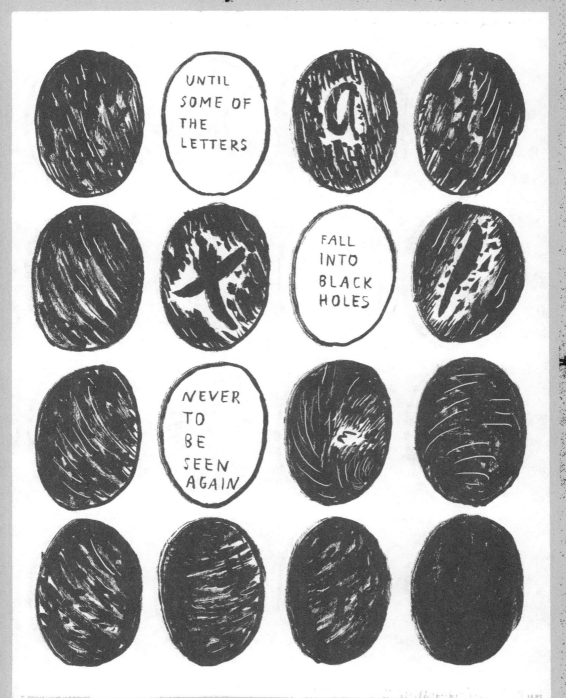

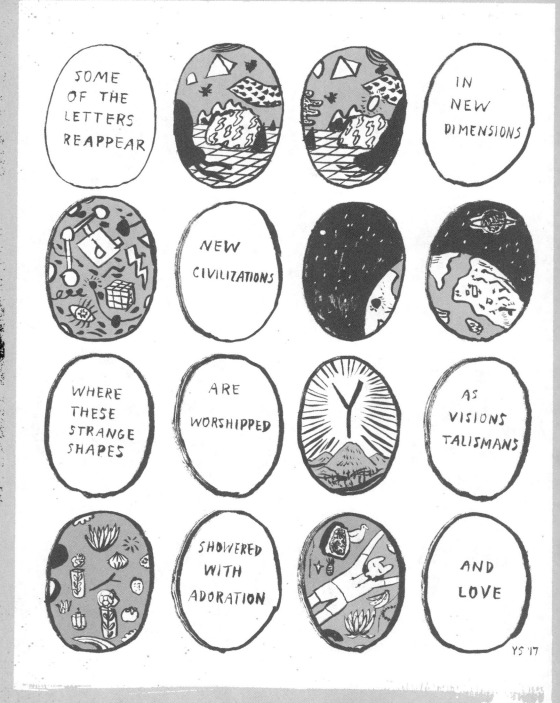

THE LIGHT BULB, THE BROOM, AND THE WORK THEY DON'T TELL YOU ABOUT

by Kelly Jensen

I woke up in a too-bright room. Clean and dirty clothes mingled on the floor, and cobwebs collected among the mess of shoes chucked against the wall. It was 2:00 p.m., maybe 3:00, a few hours after I'd worked and a few hours before anyone else would be home. I was alone, like I'd been in every other moment like this one, feeling the weight of sadness and listlessness crushing me. Most afternoons, it took hours to peel myself from bed and face the rest of the day. But today was different. I'd just woken from a dream about the pastries that were sitting in my kitchen, thinking about how delicious one of those would be right now. I coaxed myself up with the promise of sugary sweetness.

  I searched frantically among the dirty teacups and sauce splotches on top of the stove, but there were no pastries. How could they be gone? It was mere minutes ago I'd had the perfect image of them in my mind, the smell lingering in my nose even after the dream had ended.

  Inconsolable, I walked into my office so I could log a few more work hours—an easy way to present normalcy to the outside world—and cried. Of all the terrible things that could have set me off, it was the pastries my dreams invented not sitting where I thought they'd be. My body shuddered, and every part of me ached physically

I FELT LIKE ME, UNTIL I DIDN'T.

and emotionally. I'd gotten out of bed for nothing.

That was my tipping point.

After the long, hard cry and a few hours of sitting with the nonstop emotional static ricocheting through my head, I realized that I was angry at and hurt by something I'd imagined. More, it was something I was able to recognize *as* my imagination. This wasn't normal and it wasn't okay.

While it took reaching that point for me to seek help—years, if not a decade or more in the making—getting professional help was only a small first step in my mental health journey. I visited my doctor, talked about the ups and downs in my thinking patterns, then chose medication as the start of my treatment.

Almost immediately, the noise in my head cleared. My demeanor became much calmer. I felt more grounded and rooted in my life, feeling like it belonged entirely to me for the first time. My senses burst: the sun felt great on my skin; foods tasted fresher and brighter; music sounded good in a way it hadn't in years. It no longer took all my energy to leave the house, and I launched into hobbies I'd denied myself for years: photography, walking, yoga, socializing with friends old and new. My brain did not run through the list of possible outcomes of every single movement or action or interaction and then panicked over not having enough control.

I felt like me, until I didn't.

Sometimes, when I'd flick through photos I took or rounded a three-mile walk in the local arboretum, sadness would pierce through the quiet of my mind. It wasn't the same kind of sadness I'd felt before, the kind that made me ball up and hide beneath the covers. This felt less permanent and less paralyzing, like a foot or leg that had gotten tingly and needed to be shaken awake. This new flavor of sadness, when it bubbled up, never lingered for more than a few minutes. It would hit when I was cooking or when I was reading. Pop up sometimes when I decided to try a new makeup routine. Out of nowhere, it would crawl through my skin, unrelated to the emotions I'd been experiencing minutes before, and for no discernible reason. It was irritating to suddenly feel sad when there was no cause for it.

When those feelings struck, I'd lash out by being unnecessarily mean or difficult with the closest people in my life. I became convinced people were lying to me or hiding information from me. That they only put up with me because they felt obligated. I'd lay out the things they'd done that hurt me, item by item, then cut them off and out of my life temporarily. I left no space for them to explain themselves, and more, I left them no space to tell me how inappropriate my behavior was. While this new brand of sadness dissipated quickly, I'd be left having to explain why I'd snapped or been so cold.

I had no explanation.

I wasn't *trying* to be curt or cruel, but acting out sparked a strangely warm feeling inside me. I felt in control. Control was powerful, and in the moment, it felt right. It was a weapon against the sadness that kept stealing away the good in my life. But my behavior left destruction in its wake.

Maybe I wasn't dreading my day-to-day existence anymore, but that sadness and accompanying frustration was having a distinct impact on me. Though I felt the best I'd felt in my entire adult (and much of my teen) life, I realized then that my work in managing my mental illness couldn't stop at taking medication. There needed to be more I could do. I had braved talking to a doctor and seeking medication to balance my neurochemicals, and now, it was time to do the harder work. I needed to develop health skills for coping and managing my illness every single day: the good ones, the hard ones, and everything in between.

Experience had taught me that ignoring emotional signs wasn't healthy. Learning to acknowledge my internal feelings as real and valid—rather than writing them off as something silly or a byproduct of an unstable mind—meant I needed to sit with them and unpack them. Acting out hadn't made the emotions go away. It had only allowed me to continue pretending they didn't exist.

But acknowledging that my feelings were real was the key. It gave me the chance to understand them rather than ignore them or let them control me. I needed to be patient, to be kind toward myself, and to process what came up as it came up, with the understanding that not all feelings needed the same level of attention as others.

Through reflection I came to realize something about the new sadness: It was grief. Grief for the life I'd missed out on before seeking treatment and working toward a path of health.

This new period of my life, one that felt good and comfortable and yet still invited in some things I didn't like? It was mourning.

Mental illnesses make good liars. Depression told me how worthless life was. Anxiety told me it wouldn't get better without tremendous energy, and that wasn't something I had the capacity to give. Together that cocktail of insecurity and exhaustion swirled inside my mind and wreaked havoc on my body for years. There were days I was better at navigating the messages than others. But now, having named those experiences, having labels to attach to what was happening in my mind and my body, meant I had more power over my own mental well-being. Though it felt great to feel great, though it was incredible to suddenly have the sorts of sensory excitement and vivacity I'd always craved, I hadn't allowed myself the time or space to work through the emotional impact of such a chemical change.

Mourning, like mental illness, makes sense on the cognitive and chemical level; it's a series of feelings we experience, often tied to something traumatic in our lives. And yet, mourning follows neither a logical nor linear pattern. Grief peeks around corners, and it latches on when it might be least expected. But ignoring grief when it shows up only makes things worse. Our bodies and minds are always working together, but we don't always treat them as two equally important parts of who we are. It is far easier, for example, to take a day off from life because of the flu than it is to take one off because of having a case of the sads. But both of these things are valid and have a tremendous impact on how we move through the world.

It wasn't until I let myself feel grief in the marrow of my bones that I was able to process what I had been feeling postdiagnosis and to see the opportunities that existed for my life ahead. The space between being unmedicated and undiagnosed to medicated and having a name for my experiences left little room for feeling those things. I'd gone from crying ferociously over imaginary pastries at the lowest point of my illness to, just a week later, having medication that quieted the static that had been permeating my mind for as long as I could remember. I'd gone from moments of never wanting to leave my bed to never wanting to sit still.

But I'd also gone from ignoring what my mind was saying to . . . ignoring what my mind was saying. While there had been a quick change in the chemical configurations in my mind thanks to medication, I had been impatient about the grander changes to come. I wanted to skip the parts that required work.

So I made myself *listen* and examine my feelings. When I acknowledged them for what they were—feelings—it was much easier to let them go. I let myself feel sad about the opportunities I'd neglected, the months of my life when I'd sat on the sidelines rather than played in the game. I mourned the chances to grow and explore and learn that passed me by because I couldn't muster the energy to brush my hair or teeth or stop crying or pretend that I wasn't paralyzed by social anxiety.

And the sense of loss wasn't simply about what I'd missed out on in the world around me. It was also about what I'd missed out on internally: the incredible raw experience of emotion, of feeling, of the ways that the body and mind are rhythmic and cyclical and know exactly what they need to function. I'd lost touch with my inner self.

Grief was a light bulb in a dark, dusty attic. Mourning was the broom, the dustpan, and the promise that by working at it, bit by bit, that room would no longer be scary. As I let myself accept the grief, I readied myself to soak in the light.

Just as with mental illness, we don't like to talk about grief because it doesn't make sense. We want our mourning periods to have a set time frame, wherein we get to progress through sadness and anger, and then we're done. We crave a linear experience. But it doesn't operate that way. My doctor said it best: what makes us human is that we have emotions, some good and some bad, some comfortable and some not. If we didn't, we'd be robots and nothing in life would have meaning. It's when we go in the wrong direction for too long and can't course correct on our own that we need to find what helps us do just that.

Learning to live with a mental illness is work. There are ups, there are downs, and there are times when things don't make a lot of sense. But by listening to those internal cues, those moments wherein grief or sadness or something unexpected percolates, I'm able to look at what's going on, acknowledge it for what it is, and then choose to work with it or let it float away. I turn on the lights, sweep up the dust, and accept those moments for what they are while appreciating the ways I can move forward and live bigger.

I'm not a hero for pushing myself to do and be the best I can, just as I'm not weak for having sad days or periods when I need to pause and check in with myself.

I am a person figuring out how to be the best version of myself, one step at a time.

HAPPINESS GOES ON

by Adam Silvera

"Why are your books so sad? You seem so happy!"

I've gotten variations of this question ever since publishing my first book. The people who are confused about how I can write about so much sadness when I appear to be leading a happy and charmed life are the same people who are confused about how a comedian could be so depressed that they've died by suicide. The happiness someone wears and puts out into the universe should never be trusted to be the same amount of joy one has within. I once swore I could feel as happy inside as I was pretending to be outside. And because my dreams of becoming a published author were coming true, I was even surer that I would never be unhappy again.

I wouldn't be asked to write about mental illness if I were right.

I've survived unhappiness before. I have a tattoo on my collarbone to remember this, to turn to whenever darkness takes another swing at me. It says *HGO* and it stands for Happiness Goes On. Even though it took months—sometimes years—to get over the pain and worthlessness I felt, I endured, and survived. And that's the lesson I hold close to me: happiness comes again.

But things were completely different in fall 2015, the year my debut novel, *More Happy Than Not*, came out. Things were so scary for me that I can't recall a single time I saw my Happiness Goes On tattoo. It's as if this very important reminder that things have been bad before but got better with time and healing was invisible. I felt devastatingly helpless.

This dip felt inevitable. There's a history of mental illness on my father's side of the family—schizophrenia, dissociative disorder, and yes, people who have taken their own lives. It's worth noting I also deal with a strong case of obsessive-compulsive disorder (and not of the I'm-so-OCD-about-this! variety). The combination of anxiety and obsessive-compulsive disorder during a life-changing year—when I went from being a young man from the South Bronx who no one expected to succeed to a published author whose debut novel received stellar reviews and fanfare—buried me under a world of pressure. I wanted to be everything for everyone and control things I couldn't control.

My dream was turning on me. I wanted to be better than my failures and I wanted to be two times better than my successes. One of my favorite people recognized I was becoming too defined by my career and told me to take a step back, to return to being "Adam Silvera, human who writes, not writer who humans." That was exactly what I wanted but I couldn't get there instantly. My warped perspective on my career and expectations for it, both internal and external, were preventing me from appreciating the true victories of being a writer—like someone telling me they enjoyed my work. Like someone else telling me my work saved their life.

It's not uncommon for me to sink when good things are happening in my life, something I'm positive others experience, as well. That rewarding high can leave you wanting more and when "more" doesn't show up, you're left disappointed. After the book's publication, dozens of these moments eventually avalanched and left me feeling worthless and hopeless and crushed and alone despite having some of the greatest friends ever.

The worthlessness and hopelessness and loneliness I'd been feeling tenfold led me to wonder if there was a solo trip I could take to end my life. I believed deep down I didn't want this, but because the thought kept returning I messaged some of my best friends so they could keep an eye on me as I felt things worsening.

That was the first time I reached out to friends during a suicidal crisis; it was also the same night I was coming apart. I had no appetite. I couldn't sleep. My chest was very tight. My heart was pounding so hard in the middle of the night that I swore I was having a heart attack, and the force of it didn't calm down until the next evening.

I was on deadline for my second novel when this was happening and I alerted my agent so he could fill in my publisher. I emailed a mentor/friend who hit me with the toughest love that finally got me to reach out to a Suicide Prevention Lifeline for the first time. I will never forget what it was like to add that number in my phone's contacts list. It took me hours to finally work up the nerve to call. I didn't feel justified because I wasn't an immediate danger to myself. But as my mentor told me: I was indeed at risk during these very charged days, and it was important that I build relationships with professionals instead of carrying all this unchecked weight by myself. I also hesitated to call because I felt as if some of my reasons— which I'm keeping to myself—were stupid and weren't worth their time. I really hope anyone reading this understands that if your "stupid" reason is eating you alive, then it's far from stupid. I hope we can all be smarter about this in the future.

> IT WAS IMPORTANT THAT I BUILD RELATIONSHIPS WITH PROFESSIONALS INSTEAD OF CARRYING ALL THIS UNCHECKED WEIGHT BY MYSELF.

I went for a walk before I made the call. I played a cheery song and when the song ended, I forced myself to call the lifeline. My chest tightened as I thought about how bizarre the whole experience was. When the operator picked up, I didn't know what to say. But after forty minutes on the phone, I had told her so much: how I've cried in the shower with my face planted on the cold tiles of the wall; how I appreciated my trusted friends checking in on me and how I hated that I was this broken thing they needed to check in on; how uncomfortable it made me that everyone was learning how to recalibrate their conversations with me, like I needed to be handled with kiddie gloves; how interrupting everyone's (seemingly) happy lives with my own unhappiness only made me regret sharing all this with them in the first place; how becoming an author changed my life and how it didn't magically heal all wounds or spread happiness into the other arenas of my life; how I was apartment hunting in a city I wasn't sure I wanted to stay in; how everything felt lose-lose, and so much more. I wasn't rushed off the phone and when I made the decision to hang up, the operator gave me multiple resources that could better assist me locally. She also reminded me I could still call that number anytime.

I went hiking with one of my best friends a couple days later. We climbed to the very top of the mountain and drank fresh water from a spring. It was a beautiful day followed by an evening when I crashed even harder than I had earlier that week. I was convinced this was going to be the night when I died by suicide. I cried in the shower, I cried in the streets, I cried on the steps of a church. I had a fleeting thought about throwing myself into a street as a car approached. I was about to research painless ways to die. But I got it together and called the Suicide Prevention Lifeline again. The operator wasn't as great as the first one, and I considered hanging up to speak with someone else (which I highly recommend if you don't find your life valued by the end of a call), but I chose to call resource centers instead. I wanted to live and I couldn't keep avoiding local help.

When I got back to my friend's that night, I broke down so hard that I learned the sound of my cry—not the little sobs from the shower I thought was my crying at its worst but instead an agonized cry with stuttered breaths and this pain as if I'd lost all my favorite people in the universe. This was the kind of depression that made me feel lonely when I was being hugged.

Writing has always been my outlet. Whether I was exploring an idea or seeking therapy it's what I have always done, and will likely continue to do, whenever I need to relieve myself of whatever is weighing me down.

So why do I write sad stories? Because I'm haunted by those times in my own life that inspired four of my thirteen tattoos.

HGO on my collarbone to remind me that Happiness Goes On.

A green arrow pointing outward to remind me to keep looking forward.

A compass on my other collarbone to remind me to keep finding direction when I'm lost.

A series of colorful life lines representing the people who saved my life, people who I can turn to remind me of my worth when I don't believe there is any.

I write sad stories for teenagers because young adults need to see that there is no such thing as a happy *ending* when you're that age. Because your life is more than your teenage years. And that when we say "It Gets Better," it doesn't mean "Everything Gets Solved." It means you will still carry the weight from when things weren't good, but you will be stronger for it the next time you're unhappy—and that time will come. I want to show the battles that people go through. And I can't think of a better way to show young people that you can be strong enough to survive and survive and survive and survive than to write a character who overcomes their darkness.

I write sad stories so I can be a living, breathing example that someone who looks happy on the outside isn't always happy on the inside.

I write sad stories because my own life is a story that's still going on.

SURVIVAL MODE

by Hannah Bae

It had been dark for hours by the time I turned onto my street. I was coming home from one of my many after-school activities—maybe crew practice, or a Model United Nations conference, or a student government meeting. I can't remember now. My shoulders felt heavy as I thought of piles of homework waiting for me.

As I pulled into the driveway, my headlights flashed across the front of the house and my heart lurched. It took a few seconds to register what I'd seen in the glare: a face, ghostly and wild-eyed, standing sentry just inside the front door. I had put the car in park when she burst out the door and ran onto the lawn, all flailing arms and rage.

"I SEE YOU!" she screamed in Korean, loud enough for the neighbors to hear. By now, they'd already written us off as "that crazy Asian family." This wouldn't change their minds.

"YOU WHORE! THIS IS MY HOUSE. STAY AWAY FROM MY HUSBAND!"

She was only inches from my face when Mom realized it was me.

"God, you can't even recognize your own daughter?" I said bitterly in English without betraying the pounding in my chest. I grabbed my bag out of the back seat and headed straight to my room without looking back at her.

Some version of this started happening about once a month during high school. Mom, paranoid that Dad was having an affair, was convinced that "she"—the other woman—was sneaking into our house at night.

In Mom's visions, "that woman" drove a red sports car that Dad bought for her despite his meager wages as a construction worker and part-time pastor. "She" caked on the makeup, teased up her hair, and strutted around our suburban neighborhood in tawdry clothes. Mom was sure that "she" was here to destroy our family.

Of course, there was no other woman. At least not at this point in our lives. It was just me, my two sisters, and Dad. But that didn't stop Mom's delusions. Some nights she'd confront Dad, waving a heavy wooden coat hanger in his face. Once, when I intervened, she turned on me until I locked myself in the bathroom to call 911. She pounded so hard on the bathroom door, the hanger splintered before the police arrived.

It became an exasperating, painful routine. I'd be downstairs in the study, stressing over a paper on the old desktop computer, chatting online, or struggling to make sense of precalculus. Then the screaming would start.

In Korean TV dramas, histrionics are a cliché expression of female emotion. He forgot your birthday? Throw the flowers in his face in public. He's dumping you? Turn it around and berate him from across a white linen tablecloth. Shrill and over-the-top, actresses ham it up, equal parts unadulterated rage and supposedly hilarious comic relief. Growing up in Virginia, only half understanding the rapid-fire Korean on TV as I watched over Mom's shoulder, I thought these starlets sounded like squawking chickens.

Eventually, though, this kind of screeching struck cold fear in my body. To this day, I can barely watch Korean dramas. That squabbling sounds so much like the shouts I'd blocked out all those years ago.

My escape was high school.

It seems counterintuitive, since my school, the Thomas Jefferson High School for Science and Technology, is a notorious powder keg of teenage stress. In 2015, the school, known locally as "TJ," made national headlines when a Korean student's elaborate college admissions hoax was exposed. In October 2009, *Washingtonian* magazine's cover blared: "Why You Should Hate This School: Inside America's Best High School—and What It Says about Washington." From 2007 to 2013, *U.S. News and World Report* named it the best public high school in the United States. In 2014, it won the same accolades from *Newsweek*.

For all the hypercompetitive frenzy of TJ, it was also a community of mostly supportive, generous, and intelligent teachers, guidance counselors, students, and parents. School was an oasis away from my family. Neither of my sisters went there. Many students commuted from distant towns and counties, which could mean traveling an hour to work on a group project together or staying after school well into the evening for clubs and sports.

I threw myself into some of the most time- and travel-intensive activities, like the crew team. Many weeks, I stayed after school every day or even slept over at friends' houses on weeknights to study. I did anything to stay out of my own house.

I'd never been particularly close with my parents, who barely spoke English while I barely spoke Korean. When my sisters and I were young, Dad worked as a minister full-time, which meant he and mom were rarely home. Early-morning prayers, evening Bible studies, and home visits to parishioners always called.

Back then, Dad was incredibly strict, quick to whip out the Korean corporal punishment methods he'd learned in his youth: spankings, hitting us across our palms with a ruler, or forcing us to kneel while holding our arms straight up. His anger management issues and our bruises landed us in foster care for a few months when I was nine.

My mother was emotive, an artist. She had a clear, rich singing voice and, my aunt once told me, dreamed of being an opera singer. Instead, as a preacher's wife, she ended up becoming a dry cleaner and half-hearted homemaker.

Mom always loved beautiful things. I think she developed her love of fashion from handling the exquisite suits and dresses that Washingtonians dropped off at the cleaners. I realize now that we were poor when I was very young—most of our clothes came from thrift stores, and we were on food stamps for a time—but I remember a few special times when I came home to find a new outfit bought from a department store laid out on my bed.

My sisters and I barely resembled each other—in looks *and* personality—although all three of us inherited Mom's love of creating art. Once, when we started attending a new church, it took months before our Sunday school teachers realized we were related.

My older sister, three years my senior, was curvy, goth, smart, and provocative. She liked to test strangers by going up to them with a sly grin on her face, telling them that she had been diagnosed as bipolar.

My younger sister was a year my junior, but she was taller and bigger, with large eyes and a round face. She was a goofy, easily distracted skater girl, diagnosed with attention deficit hyperactivity disorder (ADHD) later in life.

I was preppy, reed thin, and short, all sharp elbows and pointy features. I was a classic overachiever, bookish yet bubbly.

As I got older, my parents fought more. These times, Mom instigated the violence. Years later, when she was diagnosed with paranoid schizophrenia, I could finally understand why she had acted that way.

As Mom's mental illness worsened, I felt frustrated by my family's inaction. In Korean culture, mental illness is an incredibly taboo subject. Any instance of psychiatric treatment in your medical history is enough to rule you out as a candidate for many jobs. It comes as no surprise, then, that South Korea has the highest suicide rate of any industrialized country, and studies show that suicide is the leading cause of death among the country's teens.

As a teenager born and raised in the United States, I couldn't understand why Mom wouldn't seek help. It was clear that she was sick, but she wouldn't even take the meds she was prescribed the few times she saw a doctor. Why wouldn't Dad make her take her pills? Why did it feel like he'd given up on her life? Why wouldn't they get anyone else involved?

All our lives, my parents had gone to parishioners' homes to listen to their problems, yet they wouldn't let anyone else know that they had struggles of their own. It felt so fake to me, the way they acted so perfect for so long when anyone else was around, only to lose control later and cause a scene out on the street for all the neighbors to see. The only way I knew how to survive was to shut them out of my life.

At TJ, maintaining my level of busyness wasn't that strange, except for the fact that my grades were less than perfect. At my school, there was this notion that you should be able to do it all: put together a bangin' Abercrombie outfit, ace six AP classes and the SAT, letter in multiple varsity sports, serve on student council, have a sweet boyfriend, and throw amazing (yet totally squeaky-clean) parties at your family's stunning mansion.

I couldn't.

What I could do was survive by keeping my emotions tightly bottled up. That way, I could hold myself together enough to maintain a sunny disposition through classes and activities, excel where I had natural talents, and scrape by elsewhere. (As I write now, at age thirty-one, I have to stop myself from saying "*barely* scrape by." I graduated high school fourteen years ago with a low-B+ average! Even now, it's so hard to maintain perspective after coming out of an environment where everyone else seemed so perfect.)

I think to many of my classmates, I appeared to be just like another one of my golden peers. I was a leader in student government, varsity coxswain on the crew team, friendly with almost everyone, a constant presence at all the sock hops (yes, we really had sock hops almost every Friday night!), and a member of homecoming court.

But I know a few adults could tell something was wrong.

In the years before I could drive, I was often stranded after activities wrapped up, forgotten by my parents, who were tied up in their own drama. Kind teachers would take pity and offer me a lift home. Other times, concerned parents would gently let me know that a check from my parents to pay for some regatta or conference had bounced.

I don't think anyone knew the full extent of my troubled home life. For all the warmth and safety I was provided at school, I was never completely honest with anyone about the violence and turmoil happening at home. It didn't occur to me that this was important enough to tell a trusted adult, and I didn't want to make excuses for my middling grades or air out my family's dirty laundry.

Part of me felt ashamed, especially when I compared myself to my affluent friends. Even now, I catch myself using the word "trashy" to describe the way my family lived. I felt like the key to clawing my way up in life was to ape my privileged peers as closely as possible: speak the same, dress the same, watch the same movies, listen to the same music, apply to the same colleges, aspire to the same goals. Acknowledging that we were having problems at home would have set me apart, and pretending like everything was okay was easier than admitting the serious, lasting damage my parents were causing.

For a long time, that's how I lived life—never really bringing up my parents in conversation and keeping my whole family at arm's length, or further.

Then, my senior year, I got one college rejection letter after another. At one point, late in the spring, I believed I hadn't gotten into any college at all. I felt like the perfect world I'd carefully constructed at school was crumbling around me.

I made no secret of how devastated I was, crying openly in the halls at school. I had thought that college would be my ticket out of my parents' damaged orbit, and now it all seemed so hopeless. I had aimed too high, and the reality of life had just smacked me back down to earth.

The rejections clashed so much with my carefully orchestrated image, they sent shock waves through TJ. Friends told me that they heard teachers vowing to write personal letters to the colleges to protest their decisions. The school paper wanted to do a story on my admissions drama, which I agreed to. Once, the mother of a Korean underclassman whom I'd never met accosted me outside the school, anxiously grilling me on my stats (1460 SAT score and 3.3 GPA) and jotting down notes so that her kid wouldn't meet the same fate. But what I left out of the equation in each of these interactions were the details of my family's struggle with my mother's mental illness.

I did end up going to college—a welcome packet arrived a few weeks late, but with a generous scholarship. It was a thousand miles from home, and that distance allowed me to thrive as a student. After college, I landed a Princeton-in-Asia journalism fellowship in South Korea, about seven thousand miles away from home, where I got my start as a journalist and connected deeply with the culture. Over the years, I began to build my success and save money aggressively, knowing that I couldn't rely on my family for a safety net. There was no room to make the life mistakes that can be typical for a twentysomething. I pushed myself to write at any opportunity, to take assignments no one wanted, to work twelve-hour days by picking up editing shifts from other companies. Staying driven was my means of survival, and it took me far. I ended up traveling across Asia, earning a living as a writer, working for the State Department. I eventually earned a spot in CNN's newsroom and made a home in New York, the city of my dreams.

But just over a year ago, as I planned to get married to my loving, smart, creative husband, we started to think about what it meant to become a family after I had survived such a challenging childhood. I knew that it was not sustainable to keep pretending that my parents aren't part of my life.

I started seeing a therapist, who's also Korean American, and our sessions have helped me dig into my buried feelings about my family's history. After years of building up such a tough shell, I was surprised to acknowledge the pain that I still carry, right under that polished surface.

As that shell has softened, I've started to feel a lot. I feel guilt over shutting my parents out, even though I know I couldn't have survived otherwise. I feel compassion for them, now that I understand more about the traumas they survived. I feel at peace about relying on my coping mechanisms for so many years, because I've finally made it to safety. And now, I get to see what life looks like outside of survival mode.

BY S. ZAINAB WILLIAMS

A WITCH'S GUIDE TO LIFTING SPIRITS

BY S. ZAINAB WILLIAMS

APROACH THE SPIRIT

HELLO??

SSSSSSS...

BEGIN THE CLEANSING

RIGHT THIS WAY!

I'LL BE WITH YOU THE *WHOLE TIME.*

EEEEESH...

BELIEVE IN YOURSELF

by Nancy Kerrigan

I get asked to sign a lot of autographs and when I do, I try to sign *Believe in Yourself* so that I leave the person with a message instead of just my name on a piece of paper. Many times I am signing for kids who don't even know who I am, but their parents tell them I am famous.

The point in leaving that message is that to be successful in life, one has to believe in oneself. If you don't, then why should someone else? But we all know this is easier said than done, and that is particularly true when you are young and trying to figure out who you are, what you want to do, how you want to do it, and the best way to get to where you want to go.

I was ultimately able to work my way through some confusing years, but it didn't come easily and it didn't come without a big support group of family, friends, coaches, teachers, advisors, and more.

I was fortunate enough represent the United States at two Olympic Games. I was even more fortunate to win two medals for myself, my family and support group, my fans, and my country.

But that, too, was a lot of pressure and with pressure comes a need for an outlet. And sometimes that outlet can take you down a path that may not be so great.

Everyone reacts to pressure differently.

I must admit, I kind of liked the challenge. My coaches often would tell me I couldn't do something, and that would just incentivize me to do it better just to show them I could. And I loved competing.

But not everyone does.

My son has a friend who is a very good gymnast, but he can't stand the competitions and throws up at every meet. Competitions may not be the right thing for him because of how much pressure he feels.

When I was skating competitively, there were girls who were technically good skaters but they didn't always perform well when the judges were watching. Some of them went on to great show careers and entertained all over the world, but they never made it to the national, world, or Olympic podium because sometimes the pressure might have been too great. They may have also known other skaters were just better, which creates its own sort of pressure, too.

Pressure isn't just athletic pressure. For some people, that pressure could be school. For others, it might be peer pressure. For some, it could just be the pressure of trying to do your best in big events.

Everyone learns to cope in their own way. The trouble with that is that sometimes those coping techniques can lead to trouble.

I have spoken often about eating disorders in sports and, in fact, I am executive-producing a documentary on that topic as I write this. And while I was never diagnosed with an eating disorder, there were certainly times when I knew that although I couldn't control everything in my life, I could control my eating. From time to time, including prior to the 1994 Olympics, I would have eating issues. Fortunately, I had strong people around me who made sure I recognized those issues, worked through them in a healthy manner, and started eating normally again.

But not everyone has a support group or one that has only their best interests at heart. So you have to be careful and have a really good sense of who you are, what you are doing, and the will to please yourself first—again, easier said than done. And it might have been a bit easier for me to focus on skating than it might be for someone else to figure out boyfriends and girlfriends and drugs and alcohol and homework and parties and college and having enough money to go to a movie (not that I didn't have to deal with a lot of these things, too!).

One of the things I have learned through my own experiences, though, is that people are strong. They are smart. They are tough. We can bend a long way before

WE CAN BEND A LONG WAY BEFORE BREAKING.

breaking, and that is probably never more evident than in those vulnerable teen years when we are trying to figure out so much.

I tried to rely on a few actions to help me get through it all, and maybe these can help ease your own life pressures in healthy ways, too:

Find something you love: Passion is so important in anything in life. If you love something, you will work harder, be more invested in what you are doing, and simply enjoy it more. On the flip side, if you feel you are doing something for the wrong reasons, you are probably headed for a fall—and that's not good for anyone. I absolutely love skating. It is why I still do it today. The speed, the performing, the crowd interaction, the physical exertion . . . it all makes me feel good and always has. I can't stress this enough.

Find people you trust: This can be tricky. It is sometimes hard to tell what is really motivating the people around you. Are they there for you or are they using you for their own gain? There are times when it works both ways: you and those you trust work off each other for mutual benefit. My coaches definitely had my best interests at heart, but they also used their success with me to recruit other students. I have also seen a lot of situations where "friends" didn't exactly have someone's back because they were instead looking only for self gain. You have to rely on your instincts in these situations.

Learn to be focused: One of my strengths as a competitor was the ability to block out all the noise around me when I competed. In skating, a lot of parents, coaches, and skaters cozy up to the judges thinking it will help them. I never got involved in that. And I still don't pay any attention to the gossip. You have to be able to drown out the distractions because they are everywhere and come in all forms. And some come with real problems attached. Make up your own mind as to what you want and stay as self-focused as you can toward reaching that goal.

`Set short-term goals:` If you set short-term, realistic goals, they can help you on your path to the bigger goal in the end! You won't always be successful, but experiencing both good and difficult situations is how we learn where we stand and what we need to do to improve so we can reach our goals.

`Laugh and smile as much as you can:` I've heard that smiling uses two hundred muscles in the face and that laughing relaxes the body. Before competitions, I would listen to two DJs from New York who were comedians; then and now, I feel like comedy is a good remedy for most things. By the time I went on the ice in competitions, I was usually in a pretty good frame of mind. As far as I know, there is no downside to laughing and smiling.

There are no guarantees that these ideas will work for everyone, and they didn't all always work for me. So I did slide into some bad habits from time to time. But these guiding principles helped pull me out of those bad patches more quickly than I might otherwise have navigated those situations.

You're going to have bad days. You're going to want to give in to temptation. You will get frustrated and not see the humor. Occasional missteps are part of human nature—and the human condition.

So remember your goals and why you are doing whatever it is that you're passionate about. If you remember your passion it can help you find and/or maintain your drive.

Most of all: *Believe in Yourself!*

CALL ME CRAZY

by s.e. smith

Call me crazy.

Go ahead, you wouldn't be the first to do it, and you probably won't be the last. That's because I *am* crazy. Loony tunes. Bananas. Bonkers. Stark raving mad. Certifiable. Insane. Loco. Nuts. Psycho. You're not going to hurt my feelings if you tell it like it is, although my psychiatrist always looks faintly dismayed when I call myself crazy, saying, with a slightly pained expression: "Well, I mean, I wouldn't . . ." and then sort of trailing off before handing me one of my insurer's brightly colored pamphlets for crazy group. (Spoiler: They don't actually call it that. I'd probably consider going if they did.)

But let's back up a bit.

When I was in high school, I was perniciously, aggressively, horribly, sometimes violently depressed. It alternated with vicious mood swings, towering rages over nothing, and an irrationally extreme response to things that people around me thought were minor. I was consumed by anxiety and insecurity. I engaged in self-harm as self-medication, didn't realize it, and functioned well enough that the people around me didn't, either. At times, it felt like I was losing control of myself. Everyone muttered things about hormones and teenagers and this all being normal and something that would go away on its own. Consequently, when I went to college at fifteen and had a meltdown, it came as a surprise to everyone, including me. I was the bright young thing, maybe a little high spirited, but it was nothing I wouldn't grow out of. I was not, you know, a crazy person.

I spent months in the dim upper reaches of the building that housed student health, dutifully meeting with the school's psychiatrist every Friday afternoon. Within the student body, the running joke was that the school's psychiatrist was performing some kind of prolonged research project, using impressionable youth as study subjects. I mentioned it to her once and she leaned forward intently, hand poised over her notepad.

"How does that make you feel?" she asked.

First she diagnosed me with depression, and then with borderline personality disorder.

A brief sidebar, if I may. You may have heard of "catchall" or "bucket" diagnoses—those that just kind of get slapped onto people without much thought. In the era when I first encountered psychiatrists, "borderline personality disorder" was often code for any young (presumed-female) person who didn't have her shit together and was probably also crazy. It was also then, as now, a highly stigmatized and poorly understood diagnosis. People who actually *had* borderline personality disorder (BPD, which, somewhat confusingly, also stands for bipolar disorder)—who struggled with suicidal ideation, extreme mood swings, and difficulty in personal relationships—didn't benefit from having their diagnosis used as a rubber stamp for recalcitrant liberal arts students with treatment-resistant *something*, and people who didn't have BPD but were forcibly labeled with it didn't do their actually BPD friends any favors by treating the diagnosis like a stigmata.

Psychiatry is an inexact science. The fact of the matter is that brains are weird, like, really weird, and we don't fully understand how they work and why. Psychiatric diagnosis isn't as simple as a blood test or a medical imaging study. It's something that requires skill, practice, and time—meeting with a patient, growing to understand that patient, and developing a profile for a constellation of symptoms and experiences that can guide experts to a conclusion in the *Diagnostic and Statistical Manual of Mental Disorders (DSM-5)*.

The history of older editions of the *DSM* is a fascinating glimpse into the discriminatory history of psychiatry—homosexuality was once medicalized, for example. Historically and today, "troublesome women" are often psychiatrized in ways that silence them or minimize their experiences, using the stigma surrounding mental health conditions to marginalize patients. In the pre-*DSM* era, a dude named Samuel A. Cartwright came up with "drapetomania" to describe a curious cluster of symptoms seen in enslaved people, who for some reason kept running away from their masters. Clearly, he concluded, they did so because they were crazy. No, seriously, go look it up, but prepare to fall into the rabbit hole of scientific racism, because this wasn't the first or the last time that perfectly rational responses to oppression were labeled as illnesses.

I'm not knocking the trade, I'm just saying that psychiatry is hard, complicated, fiddly work, and you're bound to run into some underlying assumptions that color the way the medical establishment delivers patient care. When society is racist, well, that influences how everyone, including doctors, interact with people of color, especially if you are, say, trying to come up with ways to justify slavery. If you think women are depraved sluts, well, female sexuality becomes a pathology. And so on. Over time, changes in the way society views our most vulnerable have reshaped psychiatry, largely for the better, thankfully.

That history still resonates, though: People who are mentally ill may be deprived of civil rights like voting, making their own financial decisions, having children, choosing where to live, getting married, and exercising choice in medical settings. The state may compel people to take medication, flag them on background checks for employment, and otherwise stigmatize them because of their mental health conditions.

Some people resist psychiatry altogether, as detailed in a bit, but it is worth noting that two psychiatrists can come up with very different diagnoses for the same patient, often at the same time. Racism and sexism are just two of many problematic ways every mental health professional brings their own understanding, training, preconceived notions, and cultural background to their interactions with patients. Depending on who the patient is, when they're diagnosed, and who diagnoses them, they may be given any number of psychiatric labels. Sometimes to their detriment, because misdiagnosis usually delays appropriate treatment.

And so it went with me when, in a gloomy office in the depths of a Vermont winter, I had been diagnosed with borderline personality disorder.

I was, as I'd heard people so often say, "a borderline." I dutifully went through a pharmacopeia of medications, therapy (group and individual), and a slew of other treatment options in a desperate attempt to get less crazy.

Because being crazy turned out to really suck. I'd spent my whole life being told I was exceptional: special and unique and powerful. And now my brain was trying to kill me. I struggled for years and nothing seemed to work—not uncommon for some people with borderline personality disorder, and especially common for people who have been misdiagnosed with it.

It took nearly a decade to figure out what was *actually* making me crazy, and years after that of tinkering with medications to attempt to manage it. Some people like to say "control"—I don't, because I view my crazy and myself as an uneasy partnership. We're working together, here. To exert a degree of control on my part is to suggest that my crazy can do the same. I am also aware that we will be harnessed together for life, my crazy and me—though my crazy might try to make that life shorter. Thanks to flukes of genetics, circumstances—and honestly, people really don't know; they can only offer theories—this constant balancing act is part of my life forever.

Over that decade of searching for the right diagnosis, I was introduced to the disability rights movement, and with that the notion that you could be disabled and happy, disabled and proud, disabled and content in your body and your identity. There are a lot of ways to view the movement, but for me, perhaps the most empowering element was the realization that there was nothing wrong with me. That my brain worked differently from others, and presented challenges, but that didn't mean I was irreparably broken.

I wish that fifteen-year-old me had known that. Disability can be horrendously isolating when you live in a world where you're told that you are a broken inconvenience and no one pops up to tell you otherwise. The narrator of your life instead drones on about tragedy and lost potential. Young people like that lonely undergrad in the snow-covered reaches of Vermont are often cut off from the connections, resources, and community they need to learn more about disability—including mental illness—thanks to a combination of adult ignorance, disablism, and social structures.

It took even longer for me to discover the Mad Pride movement: people who are out, proud, and unabashed about their madness—they do not say "mental illness," because what they have is madness, and they own it, and love it, and it is a part of them. Many choose not to pursue treatment, because they see nothing wrong with themselves. Many highlight the injustices of institutionalization and the limited range of treatments available for those who *do* want to pursue treatment. Don't just listen to me, though—go read *Mad Pride*, an anthology edited by Robert Dellar and Ted Curtis, all about the movement that gives you a much more lengthy, nuanced, thoughtful, detailed view than I can offer here.

In the initial years after my diagnosis, I wanted to distance myself from my brain's wacky doings, so I created as many barriers as possible. I had a mental health condition, or a mental illness—I was a "person with . . ." It was an unwanted append-age, something to be hidden away, definitely not something to be acknowledged.

As I delved into the disability rights movement, I found myself challenged to rethink the way I looked at and defined myself. First, I learned about the differences between the medical and social models of disability. The medical model posits that there is something wrong with people that needs to be fixed, and if not fixed, grudg-ingly accommodated. The medical model exceptionalizes disability by using "person first" language like "a person with BPD" or "a person with depression," with advocates cheerily telling you to "focus on the person, not the disability!" The social model posits that individuals may have impairments that affect how they interact with society, but society chooses whether to disable them or not. The social model uses "identity first" language because disability is part of our identity; I am a disabled person, a mentally ill person. (Think about other identities: we do not say "a person with blackness" or "a person with gayness," because those sound weird and are also offensive, yes?)

As I started to explore the social model, an entirely new and exciting world opened to me. If disability is a value-neutral part of my identity, neither good nor bad but simply what I make of it, and my disability is just part of who I am, and I am proud of myself and my accomplishments, can I also be proud of my disability? Can I embrace it? And, in a society where disability is highly stigmatized and people are constantly sternly warned against admitting that disability exists, can I reclaim it? Defiantly? Loudly? Can I make people uncomfortable?

Reader, it turns out that I can—and you can, too. In a world so troubled by the existence of disability that it prefers we be seen and not heard, admitting that you don't mind being disabled, or even enjoy it, can be a radical act. Disability may present inconveniences and frustrations at times, but honestly, so does being alive.

Yet, while people are reluctant to talk about disability, some are certainly not shy about using the language of disability as a pejorative. You've probably heard the considerable debate over the R-word, driven by intellectually disabled people who are tired of having a defunct clinical term used as an insult. But alongside the R-word march "lame," "crippled," "gimp," "crazy," "insane," and a host of other words that have come to be collectively known as disablist. Along similar lines, language like "handicapped," "special needs," and "differently abled," which cloaks disability in euphemism and cuteification instead of just being up front about the situation, is also viewed by many as disablist.

You probably have used disablist pejoratives, often thoughtlessly and reflexively, because they're just ingrained. You say them because you have always said them, because they're an easy way to describe a thing that is bad or frustrating or perplexing or weird or wild. But you usually—and specifically—use the references to describe a person, or concept, you dislike. Politely asking people *not* to use these words to describe things they don't like often doesn't work out well, but oddly enough, deciding to reclaim them for ourselves also ruffles a lot of feathers.

It's not just crazy people who have reclaimed words like "crazy." Other members of the disability community refer to themselves as cripples and spazzes, gimps, deafies and disableds. We have taken language that is often weaponized against us and turned it into a badge of pride. We have rolled with the punches, risen, and thrown them back. We attempt to take the sting out of these words by defining ourselves with them, and we've also used them to create a community. To find our people. Have you found your people yet? You absolutely must: they are going to make your life so much more enjoyable.

I know my fellow crazies by the language they use, and it makes us closer. I also know those who hate us by the language they use—calling me "crazy" sounds very different depending on who is speaking the word and in what context. Since most people assume (incorrectly) that I'm a lady, I get a fair amount of "crazy as descriptor for unreliable and suspect" thrown my way. Conversely, when people (incorrectly) assume

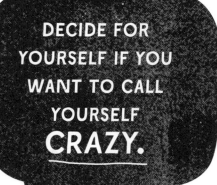

DECIDE FOR YOURSELF IF YOU WANT TO CALL YOURSELF CRAZY.

I'm a man, I'm made party to comments about "crazy women" under the assumption that I share their views.

You may have heard that you're not supposed to call people crazy. Maybe people have told you that it's not nice, that it's stigmatizing, that it's disablist. And in one sense, those people are right: Please don't go around randomly calling people crazy. But if they identify themselves as crazy and invite you to do so, well, have at it. Do it judiciously, of course, because there's a time and a place for everything and context is important. In a space populated with mental health activists who understand the nuances of how we talk about these things, you'd probably be safe. In mixed company where someone might think you're being cruel, or might hear you and assume that we are now on board with calling mentally ill people crazy whether they like it or not, consider maybe holding it in.

And more importantly, decide for yourself if you want to call yourself crazy. If you want to allow others to do so, and if so, under which circumstances. Because one way to fight stigma is to look it in the eye and control it. You take the sting out of crazy when it's how you talk about yourself, so go nuts, if you know what I mean. Other people don't get to tell you how to define and talk about yourself.

You don't need to explain yourself or justify your self-descriptors. You're a crazy person, and you want to call yourself crazy? Seems reasonable to me, since you're the best authority on yourself and your own experience.

This is a case of fighting fire with fire, of tackling stigma by deciding to laugh in stigma's face and then file our nails. It can feel incredibly giddy and intense, so treat yourself to a nice glass nail file that will hold up through the years. You'll need it.

Call me crazy; it's a perfectly apt descriptor, and there's nothing wrong with being crazy. There is something wrong with the way that society thinks about madness. We endure the sharp, infuriating pain of watching society blame crazy people for every horrible cruelty that mankind can perpetrate. Set aside the ample research demonstrating that we crazies are actually *less dangerous* than sanies, statistically speaking, and that we are at a grossly increased risk of sexual and physical violence because of our vulnerability, particularly in the case of multiply disabled people, women, people of color, and trans people. When so many people dislike you because of something you can't control, it turns out that you become an easy target for abuse.

The average age of onset for mental illness in the United States is often in the late teens to early twenties, according to the National Institutes of Health. Many people are diagnosed with mental health conditions at precisely the moment that they are undergoing huge, scary life changes. This is not a coincidence. It's also not a coincidence that diagnoses are often handled poorly and people are provided with inadequate resources to cope with a big and scary and new thing.

Mental illness is not the end of your world. Choosing to use medication to manage it in the short or long term doesn't mean you're weak or reliant on Big Pharma or buying into society's myths. Wanting to explore therapy in individual or group settings isn't pathetic—and neither is firing your therapist, if they're just not working for you, and trying someone new. Pursuing a variety of other treatment modalities, including magnet therapy, electroconvulsive therapy (ECT), ketamine therapy, yoga, and many more, doesn't make you someone who believes in magical thinking—you need to use what works for you. (And yes, magnet therapy—or transcranial magnetic stimulation, as the pros call it—is a real thing, and so is ECT, which has come a long way since the horrors of the "shock treatment" days.)

The best thing about being crazy is meeting other crazies and learning about how they live their lives. In the past decade, the number of people openly talking about mental illness—like Sara Benincasa, John Corey Whaley, hilary t. smith, Terrie Williams, Bassey Ikpi, Cindy L. Rodriguez, Demi Lovato, S. Jae-Jones, Carrie Fisher, and many, many more—has exploded. They're demystifying mental illness, making it less scary, and challenging the way people talk about it.

That helps break down the stigma surrounding the need for treatment; it's less terrifying and awful to get mental health care if you feel like this is a normal part of the human experience, not a freaky thing that freaks do. It's a lot easier to assert yourself in conversations with your health care providers when you live in a world where you're treated as an actual person. Getting help for your crazy will make your quality of life significantly better, and it will allow you to find the clarity of thought and calmness of being that allows you to get on with great and important things in your life. Those things include how you want to think about your relationship to mental illness and your own identity.

Maybe you're not crazy—maybe you just have a mental health condition, and that's okay. Our brains are all in this together, and the only way out is through, unless you have a line on a tesseract, in which case, let's talk.

Keep going.
You're doing great.

RESOURCES
TO KEEP THE CONVERSATION GOING

We can become better about understanding and talking about mental health only if we continue to educate ourselves and others about it. The wealth of resources that follows includes books, films, websites, and organizations that work to better our conversations about mental health and mental illness. This list is in no way comprehensive. As is the case with any and every depiction of mental illness, experiences and representations vary. The listed materials strive to present reliable and powerful renderings, but they can never and will never be perfect.

Always remember, too: if you think you need help, find an adult you trust and talk with them. Starting that conversation may be the biggest, hardest step, but it may be the one that changes your life.

BOOKS: NONFICTION

The following titles include reference works, essay collections, and memoirs about various mental health topics.

Beautiful Boy: A Father's Journey Through His Son's Addiction by David Sheff (read with *Tweak* by Nic Sheff; see page 212)

Brain on Fire: My Month of Madness by Susannah Cahalan

Diagnostic and Statistical Manual of Mental Disorders (DSM-5) published by the American Psychiatric Association

Elena Vanishing: A Memoir by Elena Dunkle and Clare B. Dunkle

Girl, Interrupted by Susanna Kaysen

Life Inside My Mind: 31 Authors Share Their Personal Struggles edited by Jessica Burkhart

Madness: A Bipolar Life by Marya Hornbacher

The Man Who Couldn't Stop: OCD and the True Story of a Life Lost in Thought by David Adam

Marbles: Mania, Depression, Michelangelo, and Me: A Graphic Memoir by Ellen Forney

Same Time Next Week: True Stories of Working Through Mental Illness by Lee Gutkind

Tweak: Growing Up on Methamphetamines by Nic Sheff (read with *A Beautiful Boy: A Father's Journey Through His Son's Addiction* by David Sheff; see page 211)

An Unquiet Mind: A Memoir of Moods and Madness by Kay Redfield Jamison

Willow Weep for Me: A Black Woman's Journey Through Depression by Meri Nana-Ama Danquah

Wishful Drinking by Carrie Fisher

BOOKS: FICTION

Many of the following titles explore multiple aspects of mental health, but the most prominent theme has been noted.

Bruised by Sarah Skilton (PTSD)

Challenger Deep by Neal Shusterman (schizophrenia)

Don't Touch by Rachel M. Wilson (OCD)

Eliza and Her Monsters by Francesca Zappia (anxiety)

Every Last Word by Tamara Ireland Stone (OCD)

Far from You by Tess Sharpe (addiction)

Last Night I Sang to the Monster by Benjamin Alire Saenz (addiction)

Lexapros and Cons by Aaron Karo (anxiety)

The Memory of Light by Francisco X. Stork (depression and suicide)

Paperweight by Meg Haston (eating disorders)

Pointe by Brandy Colbert (eating disorders)

Queens of Geek by Jen Wilde (anxiety)

Recovery Road by Blake Nelson (addiction)

Saving Francesca by Melina Marchetta (depression)

The Seventh Wish by Kate Messner (addiction)

Six of Crows by Leigh Bardugo (trauma disorder)

Something Like Normal by Trish Doller (PTSD)

This Impossible Light by Lily Myers (eating disorders)

This Is Not a Test by Courtney Summers (depression)

Tiny Pretty Things by Sona Charaipotra and Dhonielle Clayton (eating disorders)

Total Constant Order by Crissa-Jean Chappell (OCD)

Turtles All the Way Down by John Green (OCD)

A Trick of the Light by Lois Metzger (eating disorders)

Under Rose-Tainted Skies by Louise Gornall (agoraphobia)

The Upside of Unrequited by Becky Albertalli (anxiety)

When Reason Breaks by Cynthia L. Rodriguez (depression)

Winter Girls by Laurie Halse Anderson (eating disorders)

FILMS

Some of these films are adaptations of books not included in the previous lists.

The Babadook (mental illness as a physical manifestation)

A Beautiful Mind (schizophrenia)

Black Swan (anxiety disorders)

Inside Out (emotions and mental well-being)

It's Kind of a Funny Story (depression and suicide)

Little Miss Sunshine (depression)

The Perks of Being a Wallflower (depression)

Prozac Nation (depression, potentially bipolar disorder)

The Silver Linings Playbook (bipolar disorder)

To the Bone (eating disorders)

ONLINE RESOURCES

Many of these online sites also offer their own support phone numbers or text support services for those seeking immediate help.

American Foundation of Suicide Prevention (afsp.org)

Depression and Bipolar Support Alliance (dbsalliance.org)

JED Foundation (jedfoundation.org)

National Alliance on Mental Illness's OK2Talk program for teens and young adults (ok2talk.org)

Schizophrenia and Related Disorders Alliance of America (sardaa.org)

To Write Love on Her Arms (twloha.org)

The Trevor Project (thetrevorproject.org)

Youth M.O.V.E. National (youthmovenational.org)

HOTLINES

United States-based telephone numbers for mental health emergencies:

National Suicide Prevention Lifeline: 1-800-273-TALK (8255)

National Youth Crisis Hotline: 1-800-442-HOPE (4673)

CrisisTextLine.org: Text HOME to 741741

CONTRIBUTOR BIOS

HANNAH BAE worked her butt off for ten years as a journalist before she decided to take a plunge, quit her full-time job at CNN, and pursue her creative passions. After leaving the world of breaking news, she got married, started a Korean food writing and illustration project with her husband, brought home her dream dog, Ramona, and launched a freelance career writing about Korean American identity, health, family, and, of course, Korean cuisine. Check out Hannah's work at @eatdrinkdraw on Instagram and at hannahbae.com.

MONIQUE BEDARD (AURA) is a Haudenosaunee (Oneida) artist currently based in Tkaronto. She creates mixed-media artwork and murals that are connected to art as healing, love, and motherhood, often looking to the community to collectively explore personal storytelling and truth-sharing through workshops. In 2017, Monique received the Leading Women Leading Girls Award; created album artwork for Frank Waln; designed a poster for the World Indigenous People's Conference on Education; codesigned ImagineNATIVE's delegate bag with Chief Lady Bird; and branded the Tkaranto-based Luminato festival's opening event, "Tributaries," with her floral designs. Her collaborative murals were featured in the Kinship issue of *Canadian Art*, and can be seen throughout Ontario and Quebec. Social media: @auralast.

KRISTEN BELL currently stars as Eleanor Shellstrop in the TV series *The Good Place* with Ted Danson. She recently starred in the Netflix comedy *Like Father* opposite Kelsey Grammer, and lent her voice to the animated film *Teen Titans Go! To the Movies*. She is also working on the sequel to the animated blockbuster *Frozen*, scheduled to hit theaters in fall 2019. She is beloved for her title role in the TV series *Veronica Mars*, which she reprised in 2014 in the Warner Brothers film of the same name.

LIBBA BRAY is the #1 *New York Times* bestselling author of the Gemma Doyle trilogy (*A Great and Terrible Beauty*, *Rebel Angels*, and *The Sweet Far Thing*); the Michael L. Printz Award–winning *Going Bovine*; *Beauty Queens*, a *Los Angeles Times* Book Prize finalist; and the Diviners series. She lives in New York City. You can find Libba at libbabray.com, on Twitter: @libbabray, and Instagram: libbabray.

GEMMA CORRELL is an illustrator and cartoonist from the UK who lives in California. Her work has appeared in publications including the *New York Times*, the *Observer*, and TheNib.com. She has written several books, including *The Worrier's Guide to Life* and *The Feminist Activity Book*.

REID EWING is a freelance artist living in Salt Lake City. He is best known for his recurring role as the character Dylan on *Modern Family*. He hopes that his article helps people who are stuck in a cycle of plastic surgery and depression. He also hopes that people with this problem acknowledge it as an addiction and take the necessary steps to recovery.

SARAH HANNAH GÓMEZ is a writer, fitness instructor, and graduate student in Tucson, Arizona. She holds a master of arts degree in children's literature and master of science in library science from Simmons College, and she is a doctoral student in children's and adolescent literature at the University of Arizona. Her work has appeared in TheEstablishment.co, the *Horn Book Magazine*, SELF.com, ForeverYoungAdult.com, *School Library Journal*, and other publications and websites. She has two forthcoming middle-grade novels in the Jake Maddox series from Capstone and is always working on a YA novel or five. Find her on Twitter and Instagram: @shgmclicious, or at shg-mclicious.com.

HEIDI HEILIG is the author of the Girl from Everywhere series, as well as a new YA fantasy series beginning with *For a Muse of Fire*. Her novels have been listed on Indies Next, NPR's Best Books, and YALSA's Best Fiction, as well as among *Locus Magazine* finalists and Andre Norton Recommended Reading titles. Find her at heidiheilig.com.

CHRISTINE HEPPERMANN is the author of two books for young adults, *Poisoned Apples: Poems for You My Pretty* and *Ask Me How I Got Here*, both of which were YALSA Best Books for Young Adults and Amelia Bloomer Project Recommended Feminist Literature selections. A longtime book reviewer, she currently reviews young adult literature for the *Chicago Tribune*.

ASHLEY HOLSTROM is a word nerd living and writing in the Chicago suburbs with her cat named after Hemingway and her bookshelves organized in a rainbow. She can be found at ashleyholstrom.com and on Twitter: @alholstrom.

SHAUN DAVID HUTCHINSON is the author of numerous books for young adults, including *We Are the Ants* and *At the Edge of the Universe*. Find him at shaundavidhutchinson.com or on Twitter: @shauniedarko.

MARY ISABEL is a writer, dreamer, thinker, and peace-loving ragamuffin poet. She lives in the snowy part of the world, where she teaches, plays, and creates a quiet life for herself and her dog.

S. JAE-JONES, called JJ, is an artist, adrenaline junkie, and the *New York Times* bestselling author of *Wintersong* and *Shadowsong*. When not obsessing over books, she can be found jumping out of perfectly good airplanes and cohosting the *Pub(lishing) Crawl* podcast. Born and raised in Los Angeles, she now lives in North Carolina, as well as many other places on the internet. Find her on Twitter and Instagram: @sjaejones, or visit her website, sjaejones.com.

LISA JAKUB is a writer, speaker, yoga teacher, and happily retired actor. She is the author of two books: *You Look Like That Girl: A Child Actor Stops Pretending and Finally Grows Up*, and *Not Just Me: Anxiety, Depression, and Learning to Embrace Your Weird*. Lisa loves leading workshops on writing and wellness, and constantly wonders how someone who is 97 percent introverted could enjoy doing such a thing as a job. Read more about Lisa at LisaJakub.net.

SUSAN JUBY lives on Vancouver Island, and her most recent novel is *The Fashion Committee*. Her books for teens and adults have been published all over the world, but she mostly stays home because she likes it there. Her memoir about her teen years is called *Nice Recovery*.

MIKE JUNG is the author of *Geeks, Girls, and Secret Identities*; *Unidentified Suburban Object*; and the forthcoming *The Boys in the Back Row*. He has also contributed essays to the anthologies *Dear Teen Me*, *Break These Rules*, and *59 Reasons to Write*. His books have been finalists for the Cybils Awards, the Georgia State Book Award, and the Texas Bluebonnet Award. Mike is a founding member of We Need Diverse Books, and lives in the San Francisco Bay Area with his family.

NANCY KERRIGAN has been one of America's most recognizable sports icons for over twenty years. Nancy's rise to competing at a national level began when she placed third at the 1991 US Figure Skating Championships in Minneapolis; that win qualified her for the 1991 World Championships, where she won the bronze medal as part of an American sweep. In 1992, she earned a bronze medal in the Albertville Winter Olympics in France, and the silver medal at the 1992 World Championships. In 1993, Nancy became the United States Ladies' Champion and followed that up with her historic silver-medal performance at the 1994 Lillehammer Winter Olympics in Norway. In addition to her work on the ice, the two-time Olympic medalist has regularly appeared on television and in movies as an actor (*Boy Meets World*, *Blades of Glory*, *Saturday Night Live*, *Skating with Celebrities*) or commentator (*Entertainment Tonight*, *The Insider*, Lifetime, Fox Sports, NBC Sports). Nancy is well known for being instrumental in the creation of *Halloween on Ice*.

STEPHANIE KUEHN is a psychologist and author. She has written five young adult novels, including *Charm & Strange*, which won YALSA's William C. Morris Award for best debut novel. *Booklist* has praised her work as "intelligent, compulsively readable literary fiction with a dark twist."

EMERY LORD is the author of several YA novels, including the Schneider Family Book Award–winning *When We Collided*.

EMILY MAYBERRY is a catalyst, a change bringer, and frequency modulator. Her chosen tools are writing, art/music, dance, teaching, medicine, and science. Through these vehicles, she aims to evoke deeper feeling and thinking. To develop a depth of self-knowledge that allows our most authentic self to shine. Bringing forth wisdom and ways of living that are both ancient and futuristic. It is the blending of these two, Emily believes, that will produce solutions for some of our biggest challenges that we face today. A radical shift of perspective and way of living is called for to adapt to the current and coming changes. Her contributions are her addition to the carving of a better way. Her website is Ravenshanti.com.

MILCK has been singing for as long as she can remember. Born to Chinese immigrants in the Los Angeles suburb of Palos Verdes, she enrolled in classical piano at six years old and opera classes at the age of eight. Traveling to the historic January 2017 Women's March in Washington, DC, MILCK teamed up with twenty-five female singers—whom she had never met before—and delivered seven a capella flash-mob performances of "Quiet" on the streets. A video of the flash mobs was captured by the award-winning director Alma Har'el and quickly went viral after being posted on her Facebook page, drawing over fourteen million plays in just two days. By the end of the week, MILCK took the stage with Samantha Bee for *Full Frontal* in another riveting rendition as extolled by *Vice News*, NPR, *Refinery29*, *BuzzFeed*, Associated Press, *Rolling Stone*, *Vanity Fair*, and others. It ignited the #ICantKeepQuiet social media project as everyone from Emma Watson, Debra Messing, and Tegan and Sara to Tom Morello and Denis Leary shared the video. The initiative's merchandise benefits the Step Up chapter in LA, which provides after-school and mentorship programs for underprivileged girls ages thirteen to eighteen. Crafting "cathartic pop" rooted in classical training and inspired by a pastiche of artistic muses ranging from Ernest Hemingway and Maya Angelou to modern art, this style defines MILCK's debut EP for Atlantic Records.

AMY REED is the award-winning author of eight young adult novels, including *Beautiful*, *Clean*, and *The Nowhere Girls*. She also edited the anthology *Our Stories, Our Voices*. She is a feminist, mother, and quadruple Virgo who enjoys running, making lists, and wandering around the mountains of western North Carolina, where she lives. You can find her online at amyreedfiction.com.

MEREDITH RUSSO is a trans woman who writes LGBT fiction. She is the author of the novels *Birthday* and *If I Was Your Girl*, which received a Stonewall Book Award in 2016. She has also contributed to the *New York Times*, as well as the anthologies *Radical Hope: Letters of Love and Dissent in Dangerous Times* and *Meet Cute*. For the purposes of this collection, Meredith is a survivor of ADHD, bipolar disorder, and PTSD.

YUMI SAKUGAWA is an Ignatz Award–nominated comic book artist and the author of *I Think I Am In Friend-Love with You*, *Your Illustrated Guide to Becoming One with the Universe*, *There Is No Right Way to Meditate: And Other Lessons*, and *The Little Book of Life Hacks: How to Make Your Life Happier, Healthier, and More Beautiful*. Her comics have appeared in *BuzzFeed*, the *Believer*, *Bitch*, *The Best American Nonrequired Reading 2014*, the *Rumpus*, and other publications. She has also exhibited art installations at the Japanese American National Museum and the Smithsonian's Arts and Industries Building. A graduate of the fine arts program of the University of California, Los Angeles, she lives in Los Angeles.

VICTORIA "V.E." SCHWAB is the #1 *New York Times* bestselling author of more than a dozen books, including the acclaimed Shades of Magic series, and *This Savage Song*, *Our Dark Duet*, and *Vicious*. Her work has received critical acclaim and has been featured in the *New York Times*, *Entertainment Weekly*, the *Washington Post*, and other publications. When she's not haunting Paris streets or trudging up English hillsides, she lives in Nashville and is usually tucked in the corner of a coffee shop, dreaming up monsters.

ADAM SILVERA is the *New York Times* bestselling author of *More Happy Than Not*, *History Is All You Left Me*, and *They Both Die at the End*. He is tall for no reason.

S.E. SMITH is a Northern California–based journalist and writer with a focus on social justice. smith's work has appeared in multiple anthologies, including *Get Out of My Crotch! Twenty-One Writers Respond to America's War on Women's Rights and Reproductive Health* and *The Feminist Utopia Project: Fifty-Seven Visions of a Wildly Better Future*, along with the journals *Guardian*, *Bitch*, *Rolling Stone*, *VICE*, *Rewire. news*, *In These Times*, *Teen Vogue*, *Esquire*, and many other fine publications.

JESSICA TREMAINE lives and writes fiction and nonfiction in New York City.

CLINT VAN WINKLE is the author of *Soft Spots: A Marine's Memoir of Combat and Post-Traumatic Stress Disorder*. He's currently writing his second book.

DIOR VARGAS is a Latina Feminist Mental Health Activist and the creator of the People of Color and Mental Illness Photo Project. Dior is the recipient of numerous awards, including recognition as a White House Champion of Change for Disability Advocacy Across Generations. She is a master of public health student at New York University and a native New Yorker. She can be found at diorvargas.com and on Twitter: @diorvargas.

ESMÉ WEIJUN WANG is the author of the novel *The Border of Paradise*, which was noted among 2016's "great reads" by NPR and one of the 25 Best Novels of 2016 by *Electric Literature*. She was named by *Granta* as one of the Best of Young American Novelists in 2017, and she is the recipient of the Graywolf Press Nonfiction Prize for her essay collection, *The Collected Schizophrenias*. Born in the Midwest to Taiwanese parents, she lives in San Francisco, and can be found at esmewang.com and on Twitter: @esmewang.

S. ZAINAB WILLIAMS is a writer, illustrator, and (occasionally wicked) witch. She's an associate editor at *Book Riot*, where she hosts the *SFF Yeah!* and *Read Harder* podcasts. She can be found at szainabwilliams.com, on Instagram: @szainabwilliams, and in Portland, Oregon, where she shares space with a vicious cat named Tabitha.

ACKNOWLEDGMENTS

A big thank-you goes to the entire team at Algonquin Young Readers, including my editors Krestyna Lypen and Elise Howard, as well as Sarah Alpert, Brooke Csuka, and the countless other individuals who are part of this publishing team. I'm lucky to have such great people who believe in me and my work and who champion both.

The same goes to agent of wonder Tina Dubois. Thanks for the laughs, for the well-timed encouragement, and for reminding me it's "because" and not "despite." This book nearly killed me, but you never stopped believing.

I wouldn't be able to take on an anthology like this without the following support system: Courtney Summers, Katherine Sullivan, Brandy Colbert, Trish Doller, Liz Burns, the Ladies of BSL and ILOA, Kimberly Francisco, Andrea Vogt, Team Harpy. Thanks to Tiffany Schmidt for her keen eyes and Claire Biggs, who helped show me that I can write about the rawest pieces of myself and be confident in sharing the work. Many of you have loved me through my worst, and it's with you that I'm so lucky to share and to be my best.

Erik, thanks for letting me be me, the imperfect, opinionated mess that I am. Thank you to my mom and grandma for raising me to *embrace* the imperfect, opinionated mess that I am.

Reader: Thank you for entering this collection with an open mind, with an open heart, and for being part of a necessary conversation. Whether you've been brave enough to talk about your own experiences, brave enough to listen and love those who have, or are on the journey to finding that bravery, you matter.

I played Matt Nathanson's "Giants" on a loop while editing this anthology. If I were to get another tattoo, a permanent reminder of why it is me and you and everyone else who keep getting up and fighting, it'd be a simple, but powerful, line from that song: "We are giants."

COPYRIGHTS

JENNIFER BRISTER

Kelly Jensen is a librarian-turned-editor for *Book Riot* and *Stacked*. She's the editor of *Here We Are: Feminism for the Real World*. She loves eating black licorice and debating genre. Follow her on Twitter: @veronikellymars.

LET'S GET TALKING.

HOTLINES

United States–based telephone numbers
for mental health emergencies:

NATIONAL SUICIDE PREVENTION LIFELINE:
1-800-273-TALK (8255)

NATIONAL YOUTH CRISIS HOTLINE:
1-800-442-HOPE (4673)

CRISISTEXTLINE.ORG:
TEXT **HOME** TO 741741